The Complete
Ninja Dual
Air Fryer Cookbook UK

2000-Day Delectable Recipes with Full-Color Vivid Pictures to Aid in Mastering Your Ninja Air Fryer and Enjoy Delicious Food with Ease | UK Meas.

Matilda Weston

© Copyright 2024
– All Rights Reserved

The content contained within this book may not be reproduced, duplicated or transmitted without direct written permission from the author or the publisher.

Under no circumstances will any blame or legal responsibility be held against the publisher, or author, for any damages, reparation, or monetary loss due to the information contained within this book, either directly or indirectly.

Legal Notice:

This book is copyright protected. It is only for personal use. You cannot amend, distribute, sell, use, quote or paraphrase any part, or the content within this book, without the consent of the author or publisher.

Disclaimer Notice:

Please note the information contained within this document is for educational and entertainment purposes only. All effort has been executed to present accurate, up to date, reliable, complete information. No warranties of any kind are declared or implied. Readers acknowledge that the author is not engaged in the rendering of legal, financial, medical or professional advice. The content within this book has been derived from various sources. Please consult a licensed professional before attempting any techniques outlined in this book.

By reading this document, the reader agrees that under no circumstances is the author responsible for any losses, direct or indirect, that are incurred as a result of the use of the information contained within this document, including, but not limited to, errors, omissions, or inaccuracies.

CONTENTS

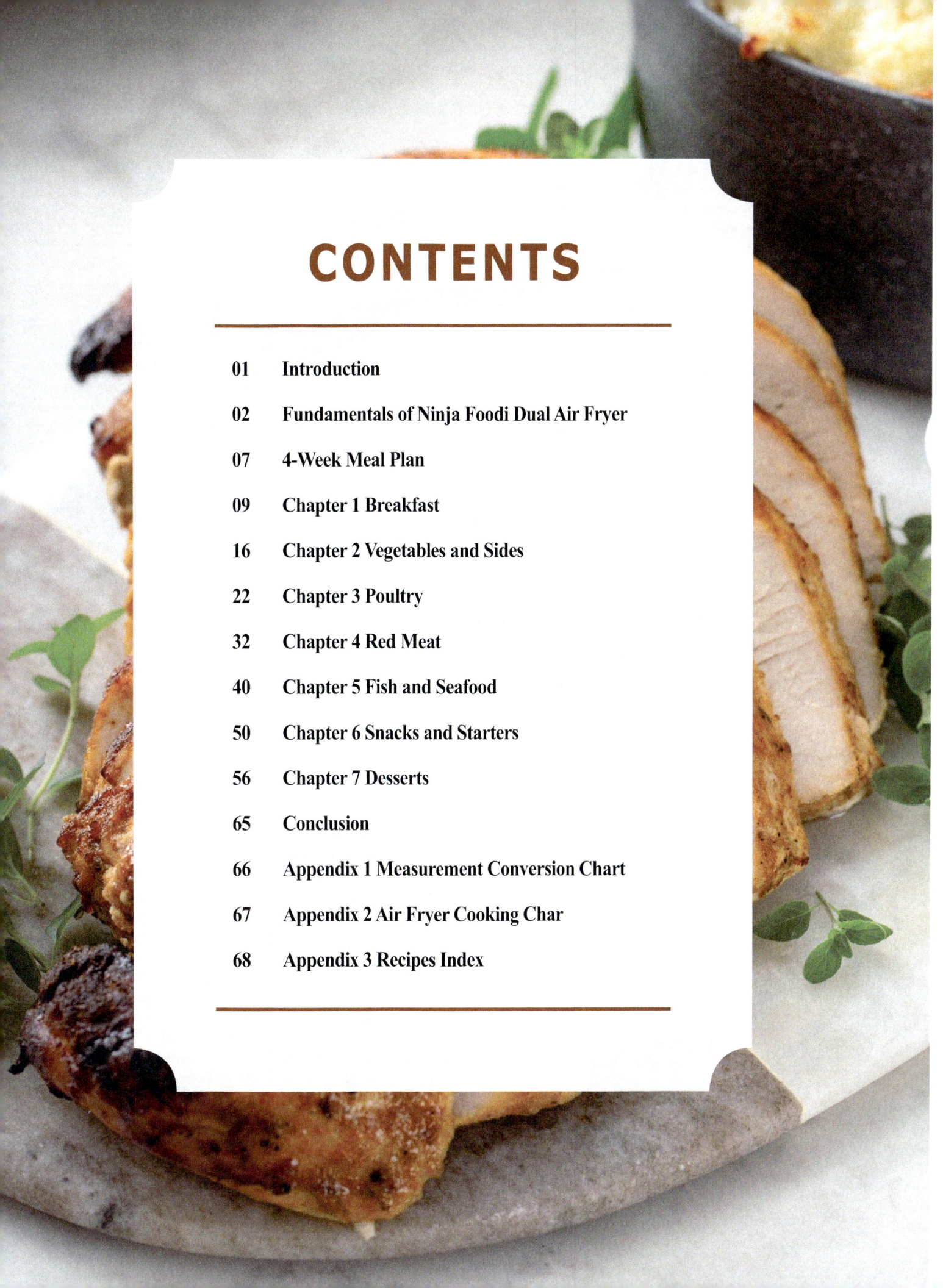

01 Introduction

02 Fundamentals of Ninja Foodi Dual Air Fryer

07 4-Week Meal Plan

09 Chapter 1 Breakfast

16 Chapter 2 Vegetables and Sides

22 Chapter 3 Poultry

32 Chapter 4 Red Meat

40 Chapter 5 Fish and Seafood

50 Chapter 6 Snacks and Starters

56 Chapter 7 Desserts

65 Conclusion

66 Appendix 1 Measurement Conversion Chart

67 Appendix 2 Air Fryer Cooking Char

68 Appendix 3 Recipes Index

Introduction

In today's cooking world, we are witnessing an amazing revolution propelled by innovation. The Ninja Foodi Dual Air Fryer is at the top of this exciting revolution. Because of its capacity to provide a wide range of cooking options in a compact and efficient form, this extraordinary kitchen equipment has earned its place as an important tool for home cooks. In the pages of our thorough guide, "Ninja Foodi Dual Air Fryer Cookbook," we urge you to begin on a gourmet adventure. Whether you're new to the Ninja Foodi Dual Air Fryer or an experienced user wishing to improve your skills, this book is a dependable companion on your journey to becoming a skilled chef.

Inside, you'll discover what makes the Ninja Foodi Dual Air Fryer unique and why it's causing such a stir in the culinary world. We'll look at the several advantages it brings to your kitchen, such as streamlining your cooking adventures and broadening your culinary horizons. Our step-by-step instructions will walk you through the process of efficiently utilizing this device, ensuring that you emerge as a confident and expert cook in no time. We'll also provide helpful hints on how to get the most of the Ninja Foodi Dual Air Fryer accessories. If you've just unboxed a brand-new Ninja Foodi Dual Air Fryer, this tutorial provides simple setup instructions so you can start cooking great dishes right away. In addition to practical advice, we've added a section answering frequently asked questions and helpful notes to help you get the most out of your Ninja Foodi Dual Air Fryer. This book is your passport to culinary greatness, allowing you to create delectable dishes, experiment with new recipes, and discover the joys of cooking in a whole new light.

Fundamentals of Ninja Foodi Dual Air Fryer

What is Ninja Foodi Dual Air Fryer?

The Ninja Foodi Dual Zone Air Fryer uses dual zone technology. You can cook multiple meals at the same time in two separate baskets at two different settings. The Ninja Foodi Dual Air Fryer features six important cooking functions: roast, air fried, broil, bake, reheat, and dehydrate. Through the MATCH COOK button, one can cook food by copying the settings from one zone to the other. It can hold up to four pounds, which is sufficient for a large family in its entirety. The two zones each have their own cooking baskets that use cyclonic fans to quickly prepare food. This Ninja Foodi Dual Air Fryer is very simple to clean. Details about it will be found later in this book.

It has a smart finish cooking mechanism that allows you to cook food with two different settings at the same time. You can make the same foods in two separate baskets or different meals in two separate baskets if you want to cut your cooking time in half. With the Ninja Foodi Dual Air Fryer, you can quickly prepare the same recipes in double the servings with the same settings for both zones. You can easily use this appliance with ease because of its simple mechanism.

Parts of the Ninja Foodi Dual Air Fryer

Air Intake Vent:
This vent is placed strategically to ensure enough ventilation inside the air fryer. It is essential for keeping the optimum cooking temperature and guaranteeing consistent cooking results.
Control panel: The Ninja Foodi's control panel serves as its brain. You can access several cooking settings and operations there. To have a successful cooking experience, you must know how to use the control panel.

Air Outlet:
The air outlet is located at the back of the unit. It ensures that the appliance runs effectively and safely by allowing hot air to vent during the cooking process.

The Main Unit:
The main unit consists of the fans, heating elements, and other important parts. The Ninja Foodi's solid core gives it the power to handle a variety of cooking tasks.

Nonstick Crisper Plates:
These crisper plates are made of a nonstick cooking surface that makes it simple to remove cooked food and clean up. Usually, each frying basket has its own crisper plate.
Nonstick Baskets: The magic happens in the non-stick baskets. Depending on your inventions, you can easily use these baskets to cook multiple meals at the same time or separately.
The Multi-Layer Rack: Although it's not typically included, the multi-layer rack gives your Ninja Foodi more flexibility. You can make multiple dishes at once by using it for multi-level cooking.

Operating Buttons

Operating Buttons 1 and 2:
These buttons regulate the results for the left and right baskets, accordingly. Each zone's cooking settings can be changed separately, giving you more cooking freedom.

Temp Arrows:
To change the cooking temperature either before or after cooking, use the up and down arrows. You can adjust your recipes using this function to get the desired outcomes.

Time Arrows:
Similarly, the time arrows allow you to change the cooking time using any function, before or during the cooking cycle. You can avoid under or overcooking your meals thanks to this accuracy.

Smart Finish Button:
The SMART FINISH button is a useful function that synchronizes the cook times for both zones. It assures that even if you cook different items at different times, they will all complete at the same time, removing the need for guesswork.

Match Cook Button:
The MATCH COOK button facilitates cooking for bigger groups or when preparing multiple items at the same function, temperature, and time. It automatically compares Zone 2 parameters to Zone 1 settings for consistent results.

Start/Pause Button:

After setting the temperature and time, press the START/PAUSE button to begin cooking. If you need to pause cooking, pick the zone and press the START/PAUSE button once more.

Power Button:
The POWER BUTTON has several functions. It powers on and off the Ninja Foodi unit, thus stopping all cooking processes. Furthermore, after ten minutes of inactivity with the control panel, the device enters standby mode, which is indicated by a lightly lit Power button.

Standby Mode:
After 10 minutes of no interaction with the control panel, the unit will enter standby mode. The Power button will be dimly lit.

Hold Mode:
When you use the SMART FINISH function, the Hold Mode is activated. The unit displays "Hold" while one zone continues to cook and the other holds till both zones are synchronized.

Benefits of Using Dual Air Fryer

The Ninja Foodi Dual Air Fryer is a kitchen innovation that will change the way you cook. It is considerably more than a conventional appliance because of its enhanced features and versatility. The advantages are as follows:

Reliable Brand:
Brand reputation is important when it comes to kitchen appliances. The Ninja Foodi, developed by a respected company, assures that you are investing in high-quality, long-lasting equipment that will suit your culinary demands for years to come. In the world of kitchen equipment, it is a symbol of dependability.

Having 2 Air Fryers in one:
The Ninja Foodi's dual-basket design is one of its most notable characteristics. It's essentially two air fryers combined into a single device. This one-of-a-kind design allows you to cook two distinct foods at the same time, saving you time and energy.

Cooks 2 Different food at same time:
Consider the ease of grilling chicken wings in a single basket while air frying crispy fries in the other. The Ninja Foodi's dual-basket layout enables you to do precisely that, making meal preparation more quick and convenient, especially when serving multiple meals.

Technology to Cook Sync Cook Times:
The Ninja Foodi takes things a step further by using cutting-edge technology to sync cook timings. This means that even if you cook two different things with different cooking times, the appliance will automatically adjust to guarantee that both items complete cooking at the same time. There will be no more juggling of cooking times & temperature settings.

6-in-1 Functionality:
The Ninja Foodi is more than just an air fryer; it's a multipurpose kitchen tool with 6-in-1 versatility. It is very good at air broiling, air frying, baking, roasting, reheating, and dehydrating. This versatility allows you to experiment with a variety of recipes and cooking techniques, broadening your culinary horizons.

Wide Temperature Range:
Accurate temperature control is essential in cooking, and the Ninja Foodi has a wide temperature range to meet your different cooking requirements. This appliance gives the flexibility needed for optimal outcomes, whether you're crisping up treats at high temperatures or slowly dehydrating fruits at low temperatures.

Easy Cleaning:
Nobody likes scrubbing cookware after a meal. You'll like the Ninja Foodi's nonstick baskets and crisper plates, which make cleanup a breeze. The ease of upkeep allows you to spend more time enjoying your meals and less time cleaning up.

Easy to use:
The Ninja Foodi's user-friendly interface makes it suitable for both novice and professional cooks. Its user-friendly control panel streamlines the cooking process by allowing you to easily modify settings. The Ninja Foodi simplifies your culinary adventures, whether you're a rookie in the kitchen or a seasoned chef.

Attractive Finish:
Aside from its cooking abilities, the Ninja Foodi has a clean and contemporary design with an appealing grey and black matte body. It not only compliments your kitchen design but also offers a trendy touch to your countertop.

Step-By-Step Using It

Cooking with DualZone Technology
DualZone Technology utilizes two cooking zones to increase versatility. The Smart Finish feature ensures that, regardless of different cook settings, both zones will finish ready to serve at the same time.
The Match Cook function allows you to cook a larger amount of the same food, or cook different foods using the same function, temperature, and time.

Smart Finish
SMART FINISH is a multifunctional feature found in this air fryer that allows you to cook in both zones at the same time yet finish at different times. This is very beneficial when you've got ingredients with varying cooking times.

Step 1:
Place ingredients in the baskets, then insert baskets in unit.

Step 2:
Zone 1 will remain illuminated. Select the desired cooking function. Use the TEMP arrows to set the temperature, and use the TIME arrows to set the time.

Step 3:
Select zone 2, then select the desired cooking function. (AIR BROIL is not available if selected in zone 1) Use the TEMP arrows to set the temperature, and use the TIME arrows to set the time.

Step 4:
Press SMART FINISH, then press the START/PAUSE button to begin cooking in the zone with the longest time. The other zone will display Hold. The unit will beep and activate the second zone when both zones have the same time remaining.

Step 5:
When cooking is complete, the unit will beep and "End" will appear on the display.

Step 6:
Remove ingredients by dumping them out or using silicone-tipped tongs/utensils. DO NOT place drawer on top of unit.

Match Cook
MATCH COOK is a mode that allows you to cook identical foods in both zones at the same time using the same cooking settings.

Fundamentals of Ninja Foodi Dual Air Fryer

Step 1:
Place ingredients in the baskets, then insert baskets in unit.
Step 2:
Zone 1 will remain illuminated. Select the desired cooking function. (AIR BROIL is not available with this function.) Use the TEMP arrows to set the temperature, and use the TIME arrows to set the time.
Step 3:
Press the MATCH COOK button to copy the zone 1 settings to zone 2. Then Press START/PAUSE to begin cooking in both zones.
Step 4:
"End" will appear on both screens when cooking ends at the same time.
Step 5:
Remove ingredients by dumping them out or using silicone-tipped tongs/utensils.

Ending Cooking Time in One Zone
Dual Zone Cooking allows you to start both zones at the exact same time while ending the cook time within one zone earlier than the other.
Step 1:
Select the zone you would like to stop.
Step 2:
Then press the down TIME arrow to set the time to zero.
Step 3:
Once you have set the time to zero, press the START/PAUSE button.
Step 4:
The time in that zone is then canceled, and "End" will appear on the display. Cooking will continue in the other zone.
For example, if you're making chicken and fries, you can pause the frying zone when the fries are crispy while continuing to cook the chicken until it's fully cooked.

Single Zone Cooking
Single Zone Cooking enables you to only use one of the cooking zones while ignoring the other.
Step 1:
On your air fryer's control panel, select the desired zone (typically labeled as Zone 1 or Zone 2).
Step 2:
Place your ingredients in the appropriate zone.
Step 3:
Set the zone's cooking time and temperature.
Step 4:
Begin the cooking process, while one zone will cook in accordance with your preferences, while the other zone will remain dormant.

Air Fry
- Install crisper plate in the basket, then place ingredients in the basket, and insert basket in unit.
- The unit will default to zone 1 (to use zone 2 instead, select zone 2). Select AIR FRY.
- Use the TEMP arrows to set the desired temperature.
- Use the TIME arrows to set the time in 1-minute increments up to 1 hour. Press the START/PAUSE button to begin cooking.
- When cooking is complete, the unit will beep and "End" will appear on the display.
- Remove ingredients by dumping them out or using silicone-tipped tongs/utensils.

Bake
- Begin by placing the crisper plate (optional). Fill the basket with the items you want to bake with. Place the basket inside the unit.
- The unit will be set to zone 1 by default. Simply pick zone 2 on the control panel if you prefer to bake in that zone. Then, hit the "BAKE" button to select a baking mode.
- Set your desired baking temperature using the TEMP arrows on the control panel. Depending on the recipe or the type of food you're baking, this temperature may change.
- Use the TIME arrows to set the time in 1-minute increments up to 1 hour and in 5-minute increments from 1 to 4 hours. Press the START/PAUSE button to begin cooking.
- Keep an eye on the progress of the air fryer while it is baking. The remaining cooking time will be displayed on the unit.
- When the baking is finished, the unit will beep and show "End" on the display. Remove your baked goods with care.

Roast
- Begin by placing the crisper plate (optional). Then, add the items for roasting in the basket. Place the basket in the air fryer.
- Zone 1 will be the default configuration. Choose zone 2 from the control panel if you wish. Next, select the roasting mode by pressing the

"ROAST" button.
- Select the desired temperature with the TEMP arrows. The optimal temperature will vary depending on the recipe and the type of food being roasted.
- Set the cooking time with the TIME arrows, which may be adjusted in one-minute increments up to one hour and in five-minute increments from one to four hours. To begin the roasting process, press the "START/PAUSE" button.
- Shake the ingredients in the basket sometimes while roasting to ensure equal cooking. The unit will display the remaining cooking time.
- When the roasting process is complete, the unit will beep and the word "End" will show on the display. Remove your roasted objects with care. You can either tilt them out of the basket or extract them with silicone-tipped tongs or utensils.

Reheat
- Install a crisper plate in the basket (optional). Then, enter the basket with the items you wish to reheat into the air fryer appliance.
- The unit will be set to zone 1 by default. Zone 2 can be accessed via the control panel. Then, to select the reheating mode, hit the "REHEAT" button.
- Set the required reheating temperature using the TEMP arrows on the control panel. Adapt it to the specific food you're reheating.
- Set the warming time using the TIME arrows, which may be modified in one-minute increments up to one hour. To begin the warming process, press the "START/PAUSE" button.
- Keep an eye on the air fryers display to see how much time is left for warming. Your food will be reheated evenly and effectively in the air fryer.
- When the warming procedure is over, the machine will beep and the word "End" will appear on the screen. Remove your warmed items with care.

Dehydrate
- Place a single layer of items in the basket for dehydrating. After that, place the crisper plate on top of the contents in the basket. For faster dehydration, add another layer of items to the crisper plate.
- The unit will be set to zone 1 by default. Zone 2 can be accessed via the control panel. Next, select the dehydrating mode by pressing the "DEHYDRATE" button. The current temperature will be shown.
- Set the required dehydration temperature using the TEMP arrows. The ideal temperature will differ based on what you're dehydrating.
- Set the dehydration time using the TIME arrows, which can be modified in fifteen-minute increments from one to twelve hours. To begin the dehydration process, press the "START/PAUSE" button.
- Keep an eye on the unit's display to see how much time is left to dehydrate. The air fryer will eliminate moisture from your items quickly.
- When the dehydration process is complete, the unit will beep and the word "End" will appear on the display.

Air Broil
- Begin by placing the crisper plate in the basket. Insert the basket with the air broiling ingredients into the air fryer machine.
- The unit will be set to zone 1 by default. If you want, choose zone 2. Then, to select the air broiling mode, press the "AIR BROIL" button.
- Set the desired air broiling temperature using the TEMP arrows. Check that it meets the requirements of your recipe.
- Use the TIME arrows to set the time in 1-minute increments up to 30 minutes. Press the START/PAUSE button to begin cooking. Please keep in mind that air broiling cannot be used in both zones at the same time.
- On the unit's display, keep an eye on the remaining cooking time. Air broiling your dishes will give them a crispy, browned finish.
- On the unit's display, keep an eye on the remaining cooking time. Air broiling your dishes will give them a crispy, browned finish.
- When the air broiling is finished, the unit will beep and the word "End" will be displayed.

Must Have Accessories

With the correct attachments, you can maximize the abilities of your air fryer and enrich your culinary creations.
Here are the few accessories which you need to have:
Non-Stick Air Fryer Liners:
These handy liners are a must-have tool for quick cleanup. Put them in the bottom of the air fryer basket to keep food from sticking and to save you time scrubbing.
Silicone Cooking Mat:
With a silicone cooking pad, you can take your air frying to new heights. It not only provides a nonstick surface, but it also helps to evenly transmit heat for precisely cooked and crispy results.

Air Frying Cooking Rack:
Using a frying rack, you can make the most of your air fryer's capability. This addition enables you to cook many foods at the same time, increasing efficiency and saving time.

Grill Pan and Skewer Set:
Want to bring that amazing grilled flavour inside? You can't go wrong with a grill pan and skewer set. These accessories are ideal for achieving charred and tasty results while cooking kebabs, veggies, and even fish.

Baking Pan and Rack:
Add a baking pan and rack to your air fryer collection to increase its versatility. You'll be delighted at the numerous possibilities of these accessories, which range from delectable pastries to savoury casseroles.

Egg Bites Mold:
Do you enjoy cooking egg bites or small quiches? An egg bites mold is a terrific tool for creating properly shaped snacks and for portion management.

Steamer Basket:
By adding a basket to your collection, you can expand your cooking repertoire. This attachment swiftly steams vegetables, fish, or dumplings while keeping nutrients and flavours.

Heat Resistant Gloves:
Wear heat-resistant gloves when handling hot air fryer parts to ensure your safety. They provide a firm grip while also protecting your hands from burns.

Oil Spray Bottles:
Using an oil sprayer bottle, you can achieve the perfect crunchy texture without using too much oil. It distributes oil evenly, giving your food a delicious crunch while lowering calories and fat.

Food Tongs:
A nice set of food tongs is a kitchen must. Tongs provide delicacy and control when flipping food while cooking or presenting it on plates.

Cleaning and Caring for Ninja Foodi Dual Air Fryer

The Ninja Foodi Dual Air Fryer is a multifunctional kitchen equipment that will improve your cooking experience. It is critical to carefully clean it after each use to ensure its longevity and hygiene. Here's a detailed guide to cleaning and caring for the Ninja Foodi Dual Air Fryer:

Safety First:
- Before cleaning, always unplug the unit from the wall socket. Your first priority should be safety.

Cleaning The Main Unit:
- Use a moist cloth to clean the main unit plus the control panel.
- Never submerge the main unit into water or any other liquid. It cannot be washed in a dishwasher.

Crispier Plates:
- Crisper plates, which are essential for that crisp texture, can be cleaned in the dishwasher as well as by hand.
- If you wash them by hand, make sure to air-dry or towel-dry all portions after usage.
- For added convenience, these are dishwasher safe.

Baskets:
- The baskets in which your ingredients are stored can also be cleaned in the dishwasher or by hand.
- Hand-washing should be followed by thorough drying.
- Hand-washing your baskets is suggested to extend their life. This can aid in the prevention of wear and tear.

Dealing with Foff Residue:
- You can use a simple soak-and-clean procedure to remove sticky food residue from crisper plates or baskets.
- Place the afflicted areas in a wash basin of warm, soapy water. Allow to soak for a few minutes to release the residue.
- After soaking, gently clean away the residue with a soft brush or sponge.
- Before reassembling them in your air fryer, properly rinse and dry them.

Regular Maintenance:
- Inspect your air fryer on a regular basis for any remains of food or oil buildup, especially in locations that are not immediately apparent.
- Take great care of the heating components and the fan. Check that they are clean and free of impediments.
- Empty your crumbs tray and grease collector on a regular basis to avoid unpleasant odours and smoke while cooking.

Exterior Cleaning:
- When necessary, wipe the exterior of the unit with a moist cloth or sponge. This contributes to its overall appearance and cleanliness.

Storage:
- When not in use, keep your Ninja Foodi Dual Air Fryer in a cool, dry location.
- To prevent mould or mildew formation, make sure the device is totally dry before storing it.

Ongoing Care:
- Maintain a clean environment by following the above cleaning procedures after each usage to maintain consistent performance and delicious outcomes.

Frequently Asked Questions

1. How do I adjust the temperature or time while using a single zone?
Time Adjustment: Using the up and down arrow buttons, you can adjust the cooking time. Simply adjust the timer if your meal requires a bit more or less time to get the desired level of crispness or doneness.
Temperature Adjustment: Similarly, you can adjust the heating temperature as necessary during the cooking cycle. You can manage how quickly or slowly your food cooks by adjusting the temperature, providing you precise control during the cooking process.

2. Why didn't my food cook fully?
Using the up & down arrow buttons, you can adjust the cooking time. Simply adjust the timer if your meal requires a bit more or less time to get the desired level of crispness or doneness.
Similarly, you can adjust the heating temperature as necessary during the cooking cycle. You can manage how quickly or slowly your food cooks by adjusting the temperature, providing you precise control during the cooking process.

3. Can I air fry wet, battered ingredients?
Yes, but only if you apply the right breading procedure. It is critical to coat dishes with flour first, then with egg, and finally with bread crumbs. Press the breading firmly into the battered components to prevent crumbs from being blasted off by the fan.

4-Week Meal Plan

Week 1

Day 1:
Breakfast: Spiced Broccoli in Cheese Sauce
Lunch: Crispy Corn Croquettes
Snack: Easy Parmesan Chips
Dinner: Pickled Chicken Tenders
Dessert: Peanut Butter Chocolate Fudge Cake

Day 2:
Breakfast: Spinach & Tomato Frittata
Lunch: Easy Roasted Broccoli with Spring Onions
Snack: Savoury Meatballs in Tomato Sauce
Dinner: Spicy Garlic Steak
Dessert: Cinnamon Walnuts & Raisins Stuffed Apples

Day 3:
Breakfast: Air Fried Pretzels
Lunch: Corn on the Cob
Snack: Spiced Cashew Nuts
Dinner: Tasty Crab & Cauliflower Cakes
Dessert: Coconut Cookies

Day 4:
Breakfast: Minty Gruyère Stuffed Mushrooms
Lunch: Air Fryer Garlic Aubergine Slices
Snack: Homemade Peanut Butter Oats Poppers
Dinner: Savoury Turkey Meatballs with Hoisin Sauce
Dessert: Mini Apple Pies

Day 5:
Breakfast: Crispy Mozzarella Sticks with Salsa
Lunch: Cheese Mushroom Omelet
Snack: Homemade Crab Croquettes
Dinner: Roasted London Broil with Herb Butter
Dessert: Delicious Cherry Cobbler

Day 6:
Breakfast: Bacon Egg Cups
Lunch: Dill-Turmeric Cauliflower Steaks
Snack: Easy Beef Meatballs
Dinner: Lemony Salmon with Chives
Dessert: Pecan Chocolate Cake

Day 7:
Breakfast: Homemade Scotch Eggs
Lunch: Garlicky Courgette Slices
Snack: Spicy Breaded Cheese Sticks
Dinner: Garlic Chicken Sausages
Dessert: Cinnamon Hazelnut Cookies

Week 2

Day 1:
Breakfast: Crispy Mozzarella Sticks with Salsa
Lunch: Spiced Breaded Potato Wedges
Snack: Flavourful Sweet Potato Fries
Dinner: Crispy Chicken Cutlets with Lemon-Caper Sauce
Dessert: Easy Blueberry Pie

Day 2:
Breakfast: Spiced Broccoli in Cheese Sauce
Lunch: Crispy Asparagus with Tarragon
Snack: Crunchy Onion Rings
Dinner: Delicious Hawaiian Butter Beef Rolls
Dessert: Coconut Chocolate Fudgy Brownies

Day 3:
Breakfast: Minty Gruyère Stuffed Mushrooms
Lunch: Roasted Rosemary Potatoes
Snack: Savoury Spiced Pork Ribs
Dinner: Crispy Cod Fillets
Dessert: Homemade Chocolate Cake

Day 4:
Breakfast: Spinach & Tomato Frittata
Lunch: Sweet Potato Fries
Snack: Easy Parmesan Chips
Dinner: Cornflake-Crusted Chicken Drumsticks
Dessert: Lemony Doughnuts

Day 5:
Breakfast: Bacon Egg Cups
Lunch: Easy Roasted Broccoli with Spring Onions
Snack: Homemade Peanut Butter Oats Poppers
Dinner: Cajun Beef Tenderloins
Dessert: Ice Cream Profiteroles with Chocolate Sauce

Day 6:
Breakfast: Air Fried Pretzels
Lunch: Corn on the Cob
Snack: Spiced Cashew Nuts
Dinner: Crab Cakes with Capers
Dessert: Peanut Butter Chocolate Fudge Cake

Day 7:
Breakfast: Homemade Scotch Eggs
Lunch: Crispy Corn Croquettes
Snack: Savoury Meatballs in Tomato Sauce
Dinner: Crispy Bacon Slices
Dessert: Coconut Cookies

Week 3

Day 1:
Breakfast: Spinach & Tomato Frittata
Lunch: Cheese Mushroom Omelet
Snack: Homemade Crab Croquettes
Dinner: Crispy Chicken Fillets
Dessert: Cinnamon Walnuts & Raisins Stuffed Apples

Day 2:
Breakfast: Spiced Broccoli in Cheese Sauce
Lunch: Dill-Turmeric Cauliflower Steaks
Snack: Spicy Breaded Cheese Sticks
Dinner: Filet Mignon Steaks with Cream-Garlic Sauce
Dessert: Pecan Chocolate Cake

Day 3:
Breakfast: Crispy Mozzarella Sticks with Salsa
Lunch: Air Fryer Garlic Aubergine Slices
Snack: Easy Beef Meatballs
Dinner: Crunchy Breaded Prawn
Dessert: Cinnamon Hazelnut Cookies

Day 4:
Breakfast: Minty Gruyère Stuffed Mushrooms
Lunch: Crispy Asparagus with Tarragon
Snack: Crunchy Onion Rings
Dinner: Crunchy Chicken Nuggets
Dessert: Mini Apple Pies

Day 5:
Breakfast: Air Fried Pretzels
Lunch: Garlicky Courgette Slices
Snack: Flavourful Sweet Potato Fries
Dinner: Whisky Sirloin Steak
Dessert: Delicious Cherry Cobbler

Day 6:
Breakfast: Bacon Egg Cups
Lunch: Spiced Breaded Potato Wedges
Snack: Savoury Spiced Pork Ribs
Dinner: Breaded Crab Croquettes
Dessert: Air Fryer Chocolate Chip Cookies

Day 7:
Breakfast: Homemade Scotch Eggs
Lunch: Roasted Rosemary Potatoes
Snack: Easy Parmesan Chips
Dinner: Cheese Pork Stuffed Peppers
Dessert: Easy Blueberry Pie

Week 4

Day 1:
Breakfast: Spiced Broccoli in Cheese Sauce
Lunch: Sweet Potato Fries
Snack: Homemade Peanut Butter Oats Poppers
Dinner: Crispy Chicken Tenders
Dessert: Coconut Chocolate Fudgy Brownies

Day 2:
Breakfast: Crispy Mozzarella Sticks with Salsa
Lunch: Crispy Corn Croquettes
Snack: Spiced Cashew Nuts
Dinner: Herbed Garlic Porterhouse Steak
Dessert: Homemade Chocolate Cake

Day 3:
Breakfast: Spinach & Tomato Frittata
Lunch: Easy Roasted Broccoli with Spring Onions
Snack: Savoury Meatballs in Tomato Sauce
Dinner: Crispy Prawns Scampi
Dessert: Lemony Doughnuts

Day 4:
Breakfast: Minty Gruyère Stuffed Mushrooms
Lunch: Corn on the Cob
Snack: Homemade Crab Croquettes
Dinner: Delicious Herb Roasted Whole Chicken
Dessert: Ice Cream Profiteroles with Chocolate Sauce

Day 5:
Breakfast: Air Fried Pretzels
Lunch: Cheese Mushroom Omelet
Snack: Easy Beef Meatballs
Dinner: Savoury Beef Hamburgers
Dessert: Peanut Butter Chocolate Fudge Cake

Day 6:
Breakfast: Homemade Scotch Eggs
Lunch: Air Fryer Garlic Aubergine Slices
Snack: Spicy Breaded Cheese Sticks
Dinner: Delicious Honey Glazed Halibut Steaks
Dessert: Coconut Cookies

Day 7:
Breakfast: Bacon Egg Cups
Lunch: Dill-Turmeric Cauliflower Steaks
Snack: Flavourful Sweet Potato Fries
Dinner: Herbed Turkey Breast
Dessert: Cinnamon Walnuts & Raisins Stuffed Apples

Chapter 1 Breakfast

Spinach & Tomato Frittata 10

Spiced Broccoli in Cheese Sauce 10

Minty Gruyère Stuffed Mushrooms 11

Crispy Mozzarella Sticks with Salsa 11

Bacon Egg Cups 12

Homemade Scotch Eggs 12

Cheese Broccoli Quiche 13

Air Fried Pretzels 13

Cheese Bacon Muffins 14

Cheese Taquitos with Cilantro 14

Butter Cheese Sandwich 15

Pecan French Toast with Banana 15

Spinach & Tomato Frittata

Prep time: 15 minutes | Cook time: 15 minutes | Serves: 2

2 tablespoons olive oil, melted
4 eggs, whisked
125g fresh spinach, chopped
1 medium-sized tomato, chopped
1 teaspoon fresh lemon juice
½ teaspoon coarse salt
½ teaspoon ground black pepper
20g of fresh basil, roughly chopped

1. Simply combine the remaining ingredients, except for the basil leaves; whisk them until everything is well incorporated. 2. Insert the crisper plate in the basket in zone 1, brush it with the olive oil and then transfer the mixture to it. 3. Select AIR FRY mode, adjust the cooking temperature to 140°C and set the cooking time to 12 minutes. 4. Press the START/PAUSE button to begin cooking. 5. When done, garnish the dish with fresh basil leaves. Serve warm with a dollop of sour cream if desired.
Per Serving: Calories 276; Fat 22.33g; Sodium 766mg; Carbs 6.32g; Fibre 2.6g; Sugar 2.33g; Protein 13.88g

Spiced Broccoli in Cheese Sauce

Prep time: 20 minutes | Cook time: 15 minutes | Serves: 6

For the Broccoli Bites:
1 medium-sized head broccoli, broken into florets
½ teaspoon lemon zest, freshly grated
⅓ teaspoon fine sea salt
½ teaspoon hot paprika
1 teaspoon shallot powder
1 teaspoon porcini powder
½ teaspoon granulated garlic
⅓ teaspoon celery seeds
1 ½ tablespoons olive oil
For the Cheese Sauce:
2 tablespoons butter
1 tablespoon golden flaxseed meal
240ml milk
110g blue cheese

1. Toss all the ingredients for the broccoli bites in a mixing bowl, covering the broccoli florets on all sides. 2. Insert the crisper plate in the basket in zone 1, and transfer the mixture to it. 3. Select AIR FRY mode, adjust the cooking temperature to 180°C and set the cooking time to 15 minutes. 4. Press the START/PAUSE button to begin cooking. 5. Melt the butter in a saucepan over a medium heat; stir in the golden flaxseed meal and let cook for about 1 minute. 6. Gradually pour in the milk, stirring constantly, until the mixture is smooth. Bring it to a simmer and stir in the cheese and cook until the sauce has thickened slightly. 7. Mix in the cooked broccoli and cook for further 3 minutes. 8. Serve hot.
Per Serving: Calories 141; Fat 12.59g; Sodium 308mg; Carbs 3.41g; Fibre 0.7g; Sugar 2.23g; Protein 4.26g

Minty Gruyère Stuffed Mushrooms

Prep time: 20 minutes | Cook time: 15 minutes | Serves: 3

2 garlic cloves, minced
1 teaspoon ground black pepper, or more to taste
½ teaspoon paprika
1 teaspoon dried parsley flakes
1½ tablespoons fresh mint, chopped
1 teaspoon salt, or more to taste
100g Gruyère cheese, shredded
9 large mushrooms, cleaned, stalks removed

1. Mix all of the ingredients except the mushrooms in a mixing bowl to prepare the filling. 2. Stuff the mushrooms with the prepared filling. 3. Insert the crisper plates in the baskets. Divide the stuffed mushrooms between the baskets in zone 1 and zone 2. 4. Select AIR FRY mode, adjust the cooking temperature to 190°C and set the cooking time to 12 minutes. 5. Press the MATCH COOK button and copy the zone 1 settings to zone 2. 6. Press the START/PAUSE button to begin cooking. 7. Taste for doneness and serve at room temperature as an appetizer.
Per Serving: Calories 120; Fat 7.45g; Sodium 1321mg; Carbs 6.95g; Fiber 1.1g; Sugar 4.1g; Protein 7.9g

Crispy Mozzarella Sticks with Salsa

Prep time: 40 minutes | Cook time: 6 minutes | Serves: 4

150g mozzarella cheese strings
2 eggs
2 tablespoons flaxseed meal
25g almond flour
50g parmesan cheese finely grated
1 teaspoon garlic powder
1 teaspoon dried oregano
130g salsa, preferably homemade

1. Put the eggs in a shallow bowl. 2. In another bowl, mix the flaxseed meal, almond flour, parmesan cheese, garlic powder, and oregano. 3. Dip the mozzarella sticks in the egg, and then in the parmesan mixture, and finally in the egg and parmesan mixture again. 4. Place the sticks in your freezer for 30 minutes. 5. Insert the crisper plates in the baskets. Apportion the sticks between the baskets in zone 1 and zone 2. 6. Select AIR FRY mode, adjust the cooking temperature to 190°C and set the cooking time to 6 minutes. 7. Press the MATCH COOK button and copy the zone 1 settings to zone 2. 8. Press the START/PAUSE button to begin cooking. 9. When done, serve the sticks with salsa on the side.
Per Serving: Calories 229; Fat 4.87g; Sodium 1009mg; Carbs 11.56g; Fibre 3.7g; Sugar 2.88g; Protein 35.33g

Bacon Egg Cups

Prep Time: 10 minutes | Cook Time: 10 minutes | Serves: 3

3 eggs
½ teaspoon ground turmeric
¼ teaspoon salt
3 bacon slices
1 teaspoon butter, melted

1. Brush the muffin silicone molds with ½ teaspoon of melted butter. Then place the bacon in the silicone molds in the shape of circles. 2. Install a crisper plate in the Zone 1 basket and place the silicone molds inside. Then insert the basket in the unit. 3. Select Zone 1, select AIR FRY, set the temperature to 205°C, and set the time for 7 minutes. Press START/PAUSE to begin cooking. 4. When cooking is complete, brush the centre of every bacon circle with remaining butter. 5. Then crack the eggs in every bacon circles and sprinkle with salt and ground turmeric. Cook the bacon cups for 3 minutes more.

Per Serving: Calories 248; Fat 21.14g; Sodium 428mg; Carbs 1.57g; Fibre 0.1g; Sugar 0.88g; Protein 12.29g

Homemade Scotch Eggs

Prep Time: 15 minutes | Cook Time: 13 minutes | Serves: 4

4 medium eggs, hard-boiled, peeled
225 g beef mince
1 teaspoon garlic powder
¼ teaspoon cayenne pepper
25 g coconut flakes
¼ teaspoon curry powder
1 egg, beaten
1 tablespoon almond flour
Cooking spray

1. Mix together beef mince and garlic powder in a medium bowl. Add almond flour, cayenne pepper, and curry powder. Stir the mixture until homogenous. 2. Then, wrap the peeled eggs in the beef mince mixture. You will get some meatballs. Coat every ball in the beaten egg and then sprinkle with coconut flakes. 3. Install a crisper plate in the Zone 1 basket and spray the air fryer basket with cooking spray. Place the meat eggs inside. Then insert the basket in the unit. 4. Select Zone 1, select AIR FRY, set the temperature to 205°C, and set the time for 13 minutes. Press START/PAUSE to begin cooking. 5. Carefully flip the scotch eggs on another side after 7 minutes of cooking.

Per Serving: Calories 314; Fat 25.94g; Sodium 138mg; Carbs 1.6g; Fibre 0.3g; Sugar 0.56g; Protein 17.2g

Cheese Broccoli Quiche

Prep Time: 15 minutes. | Cook Time: 10 minutes. | Servings: 2

8 small broccoli florets
2 eggs
120ml of heavy cream
2 tablespoons of cheddar, grated
Black pepper and salt, to taste

1. Grease 2 5-inch ceramic dishes with oil or cooking spray. 2. Put eggs, salt, heavy cream, and black pepper into a suitable mixing bowl. 3. Whisk it well, then put broccoli florets on the dish's bottom and pour the egg mixture over them. 4. Install a crisper plate in the Zone 1 basket and place the dish inside. Then, insert the basket in the unit. Select Zone 1, select AIR FRY, set the temperature to 170°C, and set the time for 10 minutes. Press START/PAUSE to begin cooking. 5. Serve warm.

Air Fried Pretzels

Prep Time: 20 minutes | Cook Time: 6 minutes | Serves: 12

2 teaspoons yeast
240 ml water, warm
1 teaspoon sugar
1 teaspoon salt
300 g plain flour
2 tablespoons butter, melted
240 ml boiling water
1 tablespoon baking soda
Coarse sea salt
Melted butter

1. In a small bowl, mix up the yeast and water. In the bowl of a stand mixer, combine the sugar, salt and flour. With the mixer running and using the dough hook, drizzle in the yeast mixture and melted butter and knead dough until smooth and elastic, about 10 minutes. Shape into a ball and let the dough rise for one hour. 2. Punch the dough down to release any air. 3. To make large pretzels, divide the dough into 12 portions. 4. Roll each portion into a skinny rope with your hands on the counter and rolling from the centre to the ends of the rope. Spin the rope into a pretzel shape and place the tied pretzels on a parchment lined baking sheet that fits the air fryer basket. 5. In a shallow bowl, mix up the boiling water and baking soda and whisk to dissolve. Let the water cool so that you can put your hands in it. Dip the pretzels (top side down) into the baking soda-water mixture and let them soak for 30 seconds to 1 minute. Then carefully transfer the pretzels to the baking sheet. Sprinkle the coarse salt on the top. 6. Install a crisper plate in the Zone 1 basket. Place the baking sheet in the basket and insert the basket in the unit. If you have more baking sheet, you can do this with zone 2 basket at the same time and use the MATCH COOK mode. 7. Select Zone 1, select AIR FRY, set the temperature to 180°C, and set time for 6 minutes. Press START/PAUSE to begin cooking. Flip halfway through the cooking time. 8. When cooking is complete, brush them generously with the melted butter and serve warm with some spicy mustard.
Per Serving: Calories 123; Fat 3.14g; Sodium 710mg; Carbs 20.29g; Fibre 0.8g; Sugar 0.29g; Protein 2.96g2.Cheese Bacon Muffins

Cheese Bacon Muffins

Prep Time: 15 minutes. | Cook Time: 15 minutes. | Servings: 8

6 large eggs
3 slices of cooked and chopped bacon
120g of chopped green and red bell pepper
50g of shredded cheddar cheese
25g of shredded mozzarella cheese
10g of chopped fresh spinach
60g of chopped onions
2 tablespoons of any milk
Black pepper and salt, to taste

1. Put eggs, milk, black pepper, and salt into a suitable mixing bowl. Whisk it until well combined. 2. Add in chopped bell peppers, spinach, black peppers, onions, ½ of shredded cheese, and crumbled bacon. Mix it well. 3. Install a crisper plate in the Zone 1 basket and place the silicone cups inside. Then, insert the basket in the unit. Select Zone 1, select AIR FRY, set the temperature to 150°C, and set the time for 15 minutes. Press START/PAUSE to begin cooking. 4. Serve warm, and enjoy your Egg Muffins with Bacon!

Cheese Taquitos with Cilantro

Prep Time: 15 minutes. | Cook Time: 10 minutes. | Servings: 3

3 white corn tortillas
3 teaspoons of roasted green chillies
1 teaspoon of crumbled cheese
3 cheese sticks
1 tablespoon of cilantro
1 teaspoon of olive oil

1. Lightly grease corn tortillas with olive oil on per side. 2. Cut a small pocket at the centre of cheese sticks and put chillies in the pockets. 3. Put the stuffed cheese on the tortillas and roll them up. 4. Install a crisper plate in the Zone 1 basket and place the taquitos inside, seam side down. Then, insert the basket in the unit. Select Zone 1, select AIR FRY, set the temperature to 200°C, and set the time for 10 minutes. Press START/PAUSE to begin cooking. 5. Top with cilantro and crumbled cheese. 6. Serve warm, and enjoy your Cheesy Taquitos!

Chapter 1 Breakfast

Butter Cheese Sandwich

Prep Time: 15 minutes. | Cook Time: 10 minutes. | Servings: 1

2 slices of bread
3 slices of any cheese
1 tablespoon of melted butter

1. Spread the melted butter over 1 side of each piece of bread. 2. Put the cheese slices on the bread and make a sandwich. 3. Install a crisper plate in the Zone 1 basket and place the sandwich inside. Then, insert the basket in the unit. Select Zone 1, select AIR FRY, set the temperature to 175°C, and set the time for 10 minutes. Press START/PAUSE to begin cooking. 4. Serve warm, and enjoy your sandwich with your favourite fillings!

Pecan French Toast with Banana

Prep Time: 15 minutes. | Cook Time: 6 minutes. | Servings: 8

8 slices of whole-grain bread
175ml of any milk you like
1 sliced banana
85g of rolled oats
235g of pecans, chopped
2 tablespoons of ground flax seeds
1 teaspoon of cinnamon

1. Mix nuts, cinnamon, oats, and flax seeds into a food processor and pulse until crumbly. 2. Pour milk into a deep and wide bowl. 3. Soak 1–2 pieces of bread for almost 15-30 seconds per side. 4. Transfer the soaked bread pieces to the oats mixture and cover with it from per side. 5. Insert the crisper plates in the baskets. Arrange the bread slices in a single layer in the baskets in Zone 1 and Zone 2. 6. Select AIR FRY mode, adjust the cooking temperature to 175°C and set the cooking time to 6 minutes. Press the MATCH COOK button and copy the Zone 1 settings to Zone 2. 8. Press the START/PAUSE button to begin cooking. Flip them halfway through the cooking time. 7. Serve with maple syrup and banana slices.

Chapter 2 Vegetables and Sides

Easy Roasted Broccoli with Spring Onions 17

Garlicky Mushrooms with Parsley 17

Roasted Rosemary Potatoes 17

Corn on the Cob 18

Sweet Potato Fries 18

Air Fryer Garlic Aubergine Slices 18

Dill-Turmeric Cauliflower Steaks 19

Garlicky Courgette Slices 19

Crispy Asparagus with Tarragon.. 19

Spiced Breaded Potato Wedges 20

Roasted Butternut Squash and Mushrooms with Cranberries 20

Cheese Mushroom Omelet 21

Crispy Corn Croquettes 21

Easy Roasted Broccoli with Spring Onions

Prep time: 5 minutes | Cook time: 15 minutes | Serves: 4

455g broccoli, roughly chopped
1 tablespoon olive oil
1 teaspoon salt
50g spring onions, chopped

1. Mix broccoli with olive oil and salt. 2. Insert the crisper plate in the basket in zone 1, and transfer the mixture to it. 3. Select AIR FRY mode, adjust the cooking temperature to 185°C and set the cooking time to 15 minutes. 4. Press the START/PAUSE button to begin cooking. 5. Flip them after 5 minutes of cooking time. 6. After 10 minutes of cooking time, sprinkle the broccoli with spring onions. 7. Serve hot.
Per Serving: Calories 59; Fat 3.96g; Sodium 621mg; Carbs 4.27g; Fibre 3.4g; Sugar 0.76g; Protein 3.85g

Garlicky Mushrooms with Parsley

Prep Time: 15 minutes. | Cook Time: 12 minutes. | Servings: 2

225g mushrooms, sliced
1 tablespoon parsley, chopped
1 teaspoon soy sauce
½ teaspoon garlic powder
1 tablespoon olive oil
Black pepper
Salt

1. Add all the recipe ingredients into the mixing bowl and toss well. 2. Install a crisper plate in the Zone 1 basket and place the mushrooms inside. Then, insert the basket in the unit. Select Zone 1, select AIR FRY, set the temperature to 195°C, and set the time for 12 minutes. Press START/PAUSE to begin cooking. Shake the basket halfway through. 3. Serve and enjoy.

Roasted Rosemary Potatoes

Prep time: 10 minutes | Cook time: 6 minutes | Serves: 4

3 large red potatoes, cubed
¼ teaspoon ground rosemary
¼ teaspoon ground thyme
⅛ teaspoon salt
⅛ teaspoon ground black pepper
2 teaspoons extra-light olive oil

1. Place potatoes in large bowl and sprinkle them with rosemary, thyme, salt, and pepper, stir them to coat the potatoes well. 2. Coat the potatoes with oil. 3. Insert the crisper plates in the baskets. Divide the potatoes between the baskets in zone 1 and zone 2. 4. Select AIR FRY mode, adjust the cooking temperature to 165°C and set the cooking time to 6 minutes. 5. Press the MATCH COOK button and copy the zone 1 settings to zone 2. 6. Press the START/PAUSE button to begin cooking. 7. Stir the potatoes after 4 minutes of cooking time. 8. Serve hot.
Per Serving: Calories 214; Fat 2.64g; Sodium 127mg; Carbs 44.17g; Fibre 4.7g; Sugar 3.65g; Protein 5.26g

Chapter 2 Vegetables and Sides

Corn on the Cob

Prep time: 5 minutes | Cook time: 15 minutes | Serves: 4

2 large ears fresh corn
Olive oil for misting
Salt (optional)

1. Shuck corn, remove silks, and wash. 2. Cut or break each ear in half crosswise. 3. Spray corn with olive oil. 4. Insert the crisper plate in the basket in zone 1, and transfer the food to it. 5. Select AIR FRY mode, adjust the cooking temperature to 200°C and set the cooking time to 15 minutes. 6. Press the START/PAUSE button to begin cooking. 7. Serve plain or with coarsely ground salt.
Per Serving: Calories 81; Fat 3.09g; Sodium 127mg; Carbs 13.6g; Fiber 1.9g; Sugar 2.3g; Protein 2.3g

Sweet Potato Fries

Prep time: 15 minutes | Cook time: 30 minutes | Serves: 4

900g sweet potatoes
1 teaspoon dried marjoram
2 teaspoons olive oil
Sea salt

1. Peel and cut the potatoes into ½ cm sticks, 10 to 12 cm long. 2. In a sealable plastic bag or bowl with lid, toss sweet potatoes with marjoram and olive oil. Rub seasonings in to coat well. 3. Insert the crisper plate in the basket in zone 1, and transfer the sweet potatoes to it. 4. Select AIR FRY mode, adjust the cooking temperature to 200°C and set the cooking time to 30 minutes. 5. Press the START/PAUSE button to begin cooking. 6. There will be some brown spots on edges when cooked. 7. Season the food with sea salt before serving.
Per Serving: Calories 195; Fat 2.46g; Sodium 53mg; Carbs 39.71g; Fibre 5.1g; Sugar 1.78g; Protein 4.6g

Air Fryer Garlic Aubergine Slices

Prep Time: 15 minutes | Cook Time: 14 minutes | Serves: 2

1 large aubergine, trimmed, peeled
1 teaspoon salt
1 teaspoon minced garlic
Cooking spray

1. Slice the aubergine and sprinkle with salt, minced garlic, and cooking spray. 2. Install a crisper plate in the Zone 1 basket. 3. Then put the aubergine slices in the basket and insert the basket in the unit. 4. Select Zone 1, select AIR FRY, set the temperature to 175°C, and set the time for 14 minutes. Press START/PAUSE to begin cooking. Flipping halfway through the cooking time. 5. When cooking is complete, serve immediately
Per Serving: Calories 71; Fat 0.5g; Sodium 1168mg; Carbs 16.57g; Fibre 8.2g; Sugar 9.69g; Protein 2.77g

Chapter 2 Vegetables and Sides

Dill-Turmeric Cauliflower Steaks

Prep Time: 10 minutes | Cook Time: 14 minutes | Serves: 4

675 g cauliflower head
1 tablespoon sesame oil
1 teaspoon ground turmeric
1 teaspoon dried dill

1. Cut the cauliflower into the steaks and place in a mixing bowl. Sprinkle with dill, ground turmeric, and sesame oil. 2. Install a crisper plate in the Zone 1 basket. 3. Put the steaks in the basket and insert the basket in the unit. 4. Select Zone 1, select AIR FRY, set the temperature to 185°C, and set the time for 14 minutes. Press START/PAUSE to begin cooking. 5. Flipping halfway through the cooking time. 6. When cooking is complete, serve immediately.
Per Serving: Calories 77; Fat 3.98g; Sodium 51mg; Carbs 9.25g; Fibre 3.7g; Sugar 3.27g; Protein 3.42g

Garlicky Courgette Slices

Prep Time: 10 minutes | Cook Time: 6 minutes | Serves: 4

3 large courgettes, sliced
1 tablespoon minced garlic
2 tablespoons sesame oil

1. Install a crisper plate in both baskets. 2. In a small bowl, mix the sesame oil with the minced garlic. 3. Then brush the courgette slices with the garlic mixture and put them evenly in the baskets. Then insert the baskets in the unit. 4. Select Zone 1, select AIR FRY, set the temperature to 205°C, and set time to 6 minutes. Select MATCH COOK to match Zone 2 settings to Zone 1. Press the START/PAUSE button to begin cooking. Flipping halfway through the cooking time. 5. When cooking is complete, serve immediately.
Per Serving: Calories 66; Fat 6.86g; Sodium 1mg; Carbs 1.08g; Fibre 0.2g; Sugar 0.02g; Protein 0.46g

Crispy Asparagus with Tarragon

Prep Time: 5 minutes | Cook Time: 10 minutes | Serves: 4

1 bunch asparagus (455 g), washed and trimmed
⅛ teaspoon dried tarragon, crushed
Salt and pepper
1 to 2 teaspoons extra-light olive oil

1. Place the asparagus spears on a cutting board and sprinkle with tarragon, salt, and pepper. 2. Drizzle with 1 teaspoon of oil and roll the spears or mix by your hand. Add more oil if necessary. 3. Install a crisper plate in both baskets. Place the spears evenly in the 2 baskets. Then insert the baskets in the unit. 4. Select Zone 1, select AIR FRY, set the temperature to 200°C, and set time to 5 minutes. Select MATCH COOK to match Zone 2 settings to Zone 1. Press the START/PAUSE button to begin cooking. 5. Shake basket or stir spears with a spoon. 6. Cook for an additional 4 to 5 minutes or just until crisp-tender.
Per Serving: Calories 37; Fat 1.3g; Sodium 46mg; Carbs 5.53g; Fibre 2.6g; Sugar 2.93g; Protein 2.67g

Spiced Breaded Potato Wedges

Prep time: 5 minutes | Cook time: 15 minutes | Serves: 3-4

455g medium Yukon gold potatoes
½ teaspoon cayenne pepper
½ teaspoon thyme
½ teaspoon garlic powder
½ teaspoon salt
½ teaspoon smoked paprika
100g dry breadcrumbs
Oil for misting or cooking spray

1. Wash potatoes, cut them into thick wedges, and drop wedges into a bowl of water to prevent browning. 2. Mix the potato wedges with the cayenne pepper, thyme, garlic powder, salt, paprika, and breadcrumbs and spread on a sheet of wax paper. 3. Remove potatoes from water and, without drying them, roll in the breadcrumb mixture. 4. Insert the crisper plates in the baskets. Divide the potato wedges between the baskets in zone 1 and zone 2. 5. Select AIR FRY mode, adjust the cooking temperature to 200°C and set the cooking time to 15 minutes. 6. Press the MATCH COOK button and copy the zone 1 settings to zone 2. 7. Press the START/PAUSE button to begin cooking. 8. Toss the potato wedges halfway through cooking. You can cook them longer.
Per Serving: Calories 190; Fat 1.57g; Sodium 481mg; Carbs 38.49g; Fiber 3.8g; Sugar 2.5g; Protein 5.78g

Roasted Butternut Squash and Mushrooms with Cranberries

Prep Time: 15 minutes. | Cook Time: 30 minutes. | Servings: 6

820g butternut squash, diced
30g dried cranberries
3 garlic cloves, minced
1 tablespoon soy sauce
1 tablespoon balsamic vinegar
1 tablespoon olive oil
225g mushrooms, quartered
110g green onions, sliced

1. In a suitable mixing bowl, mix together squash, mushrooms, and green onion and set aside. 2. In another bowl, whisk together oil, garlic, vinegar, and soy sauce. 3. Pour oil mixture over squash and toss to coat. 4. Install a crisper plate in the Zone 1 basket and grease it with cooking spray. Place the squash mixture inside. Then, insert the basket in the unit. Select Zone 1, select AIR FRY, set the temperature to 200°C, and set the time for 30 minutes. Press START/PAUSE to begin cooking. Shake after every 5 minutes. 5. Toss with cranberries and serve hot.

Cheese Mushroom Omelet

Prep Time: 15 minutes | Cook Time: 35 minutes | Serves: 2

3 button mushrooms, thinly sliced
1 lemongrass, chopped
½ teaspoon dried marjoram
5 eggs
35 g Swiss cheese, grated
2 tablespoons sour cream
1½ teaspoon dried rosemary
2 teaspoons red pepper flakes, crushed
2 tablespoons butter, melted
½ red onion, peeled and sliced into thin rounds
½ teaspoon garlic powder
1 teaspoon dried dill weed
Fine sea salt and ground black pepper, to your liking

1. Melt the margarine in a frying pan over medium heat. Then, sauté the onion, lemongrass and mushrooms until they have softened; reserve. 2. Whisk the eggs in a mixing bowl, fold in the sour cream and stir well. 3. Stir in the red pepper, garlic powder, salt, black pepper, rosemary, marjoram, and dill. 4. Grease a baking dish with a thin layer of a cooking spray. Pour the egg mixture into the baking dish; add in the reserved mixture. Add the Swiss cheese on top. 5. Place the baking dish in the Zone 1 basket and insert the basket in the unit. Select Zone 1, select BAKE, set the temperature to 160°C, and set the time for 35 minutes. Press START/PAUSE to begin cooking. 6. Cook until a knife inserted in the centre comes out clean and dry.
Per Serving: Calories 616; Fat 44g; Sodium 416mg; Carbs 22.29g; Fibre 5.8g; Sugar 5.81g; Protein 37g

Crispy Corn Croquettes

Prep time: 10 minutes | Cook time: 15 minutes | Serves: 4

125g leftover mashed potatoes
330g corn kernels (if frozen, thawed, and well drained)
¼ teaspoon onion powder
⅛ teaspoon ground black pepper
¼ teaspoon salt
55g panko breadcrumbs
Oil for misting or cooking spray

1. Place the potatoes and half the corn in food processor and pulse until corn is well chopped. 2. Transfer mixture to large bowl and stir in remaining corn, onion powder, pepper and salt. 3. Shape the mixture into 16 balls. 4. Roll balls in panko crumbs and mist them with oil or cooking spray. 5. Insert the crisper plates in the baskets and line them with parchment paper. Divide the balls between the baskets in zone 1 and zone 2. 6. Select AIR FRY mode, adjust the cooking temperature to 180°C and set the cooking time to 15 minutes. 7. Press the MATCH COOK button and copy the zone 1 settings to zone 2. 8. Press the START/PAUSE button to begin cooking. 9. When done, the balls should be golden brown and crispy.
Per Serving: Calories 146; Fat 1.18g; Sodium 252mg; Carbs 31.77g; Fiber 3.3g; Sugar 3.76g; Protein 4.78g

Chapter 3 Poultry

Pickled Chicken Tenders 23

Crispy Chicken Fillets 23

Crunchy Chicken Nuggets 24

Crispy Chicken Tenders 24

Delicious Herb Roasted Whole Chicken 25

Tasty Lime Garlic Chicken Wings 25

Lemon Rosemary Chicken Wings 26

Herbed Turkey Breast 26

Lime Chicken Breast with Parsley 27

Garlic Chicken Sausages 27

Spicy Coconut Chicken Strips 28

Cheese & Pork Rinds-Crusted Chicken Breast 28

Savoury Turkey Meatballs with Hoisin Sauce 29

Crispy Chicken Cutlets with Lemon-Caper Sauce 30

Cornflake-Crusted Chicken Drumsticks 31

Pickled Chicken Tenders

Prep Time: 15 minutes | Cook Time: 12 minutes | Serves: 4

12 chicken tenders
300 ml dill pickle juice, plus more if needed
1 large egg
1 large egg white
½ teaspoon salt
Freshly ground black pepper
50 g seasoned bread crumbs, regular or gluten-free
55 g seasoned panko bread crumbs, regular or gluten-free
Olive oil spray

1. In a shallow bowl, place the chicken and cover with the pickle juice. Cover and marinate for 8 hours in the fridge. 2. Drain the chicken and pat dry with paper towels. 3. Whisk the whole egg, egg white, salt, and pepper in a medium bowl. In another shallow bowl, combine both bread crumbs. 4. One piece at a time, dip the chicken in the egg mix, then dredge into the bread crumbs. Shake off any excess and place on a work surface. Spray both sides of the chicken with oil. 5. Install a crisper plate in both baskets. Place the chicken in a single layer in both baskets. Then insert the baskets in unit. 6. Select Zone 1, select AIR FRY, set the temperature to 205°C, and set time to 12 minutes. Select MATCH COOK to match Zone 2 settings to Zone 1. Press the START/PAUSE button to begin cooking. 7. Flip halfway through the cooking time. Cook until crispy and golden. Serve immediately.

Per Serving: Calories 214; Fat 6.53g; Sodium 817mg; Carbs 5.76g; Fibre 0.7g; Sugar 1.06g; Protein 31.41g

Crispy Chicken Fillets

Prep Time: 10 minutes | Cook Time: 6 minutes | Serves: 3

8 pieces of chicken fillet [approximately 3 x 2.5 cm x 2.5 cm dimensions]
1 egg
25 g salted butter, melted
100 g friendly bread crumbs
1 tsp. garlic powder
50 g parmesan cheese
1 tsp. Italian herbs

1. Whisk together the egg, garlic powder, melted butter, and Italian herbs in a large bowl and add the chicken pieces. Toss to coat well. Allow to marinate for 10 minutes. 2. In a separate bowl, mix up the Panko bread crumbs and parmesan. Coat the marinated chicken in the panko mixture. 3. Install a crisper plate in both baskets and line them with aluminum foil. Place the coated chicken pieces evenly in both baskets and inserts basket in the unit. 4. Select Zone 1, select AIR FRY, set the temperature to 200°C, and set the time to 6 minutes. Select MATCH COOK to match Zone 2 settings to Zone 1. Press the START/PAUSE button to begin cooking. 5. Serve the chicken fillets hot.

Per Serving: Calories 461; Fat 17.98g; Sodium 601mg; Carbs 8.95g; Fibre 0.4g; Sugar 0.76g; Protein 62.31g

Crunchy Chicken Nuggets

Prep Time: 15 minutes | Cook Time: 10 minutes | Serves: 4

225 g chicken breast, cut into pieces
1 tsp. parsley
1 tsp. paprika
1 tbsp. olive oil
2 eggs, beaten
1 tsp. tomato ketchup
1 tsp. garlic, minced
50 g friendly bread crumbs
Pepper and salt to taste

1. Mix together the bread crumbs, paprika, olive oil, pepper, and salt in a bowl. 2. Whisk the eggs in another bowl. 3. Pulse the chicken, ketchup, one egg, garlic, and parsley in a food processor. 4. Shape equal amounts of the pureed chicken mix into nuggets. Dip each one in the egg and then dredge in the bread crumb mix. 5. Install a crisper plate in the Zone 1 basket. Place the coated chicken nuggets in the basket and insert the basket in the unit. 6. Select Zone 1, select AIR FRY, set the temperature to 200°C, and set time for 10 minutes. Press START/PAUSE to begin cooking. Serve the nuggets hot.
Per Serving: Calories 212; Fat 13.7g; Sodium 110mg; Carbs 4.45g; Fibre 0.5g; Sugar 1.32g; Protein 17.09g

Crispy Chicken Tenders

Prep Time: 15 minutes | Cook Time: 14 minutes | Serves: 4

900 g skinless and boneless chicken tenders
3 large eggs
6 tbsp. skimmed milk
60 g flour
100 g friendly bread crumbs
¼ tsp. black pepper
1 tsp. salt
2 tbsp. olive oil

1. Combine the bread crumbs and olive oil in a large bowl. 2. Whisk together the eggs and milk in a separate bowl and sprinkle with salt and black pepper. 3. Place the flour in a third bowl. 4. Cut the chicken tenders into 2.5 cm strips. Dredge each piece of chicken in the flour, then dip into the egg mixture, finally roll in the bread crumbs. 5. Install a crisper plate in the Zone 1 basket. Place the coated chicken tenders in the basket and insert the basket in the unit. 6. Select Zone 1, select AIR FRY, set the temperature to 195°C, and set time for 14 minutes. Press START/PAUSE to begin cooking. 7. Toss the food a few times during the cooking process to ensure they turn crispy. 8. Serve with mashed potatoes and a dipping sauce if desired.
Per Serving: Calories 467; Fat 17.26g; Sodium 743mg; Carbs 17.89g; Fibre 0.7g; Sugar 1.75g; Protein 56.17g

Delicious Herb Roasted Whole Chicken

Prep Time: 15 minutes | Cook Time: 38 minutes | Serves: 4

2.2 kg – 3.1 kg whole chicken with skin
1 tsp. garlic powder
1 tsp. onion powder
½ tsp. dried thyme
½ tsp. dried basil
½ tsp. dried rosemary
½ tsp. black pepper
2 tsp. salt
2 tbsp. extra virgin olive oil

1. Rub the chicken with salt, herbs, pepper, olive oil and other seasonings on all sides. Allow to marinade for at least 20 – 30 minutes. 2. Install a crisper plate in the Zone 1 basket. Place the marinated chicken in the basket and insert the basket in the unit. 3. Select Zone 1, select AIR FRY, set the temperature to 170°C, and set time for 18 minutes. Press START/PAUSE to begin cooking. 4. When cooking time is up, flip the chicken over and cook for 20 more minutes. 5. Allow the chicken to rest for 10 minutes before carving and serving.
Per Serving: Calories 1285; Fat 92.18g; Sodium 1561mg; Carbs 1.37g; Fibre 0.3g; Sugar 0.06g; Protein 105.72g

Tasty Lime Garlic Chicken Wings

Prep Time: 15 minutes | Cook Time: 15 minutes | Serves: 6

1.8 kg chicken wings
6 tbsp. red wine vinegar
6 tbsp. lime juice
1 tsp. fresh ginger, minced
1 tbsp. sugar
1 tsp. thyme, chopped
½ tsp. white pepper
¼ tsp. ground cinnamon
1 habanero pepper, chopped
6 garlic cloves, chopped
2 tbsp. soy sauce
2½ tbsp. olive oil
¼ tsp. salt

1. In a bowl, combine all the ingredients and mix well, ensuring to coat the chicken evenly. 2. Then marinate the chicken in the fridge for 1 hour. 3. Install a crisper plate in both baskets. Place the marinated chicken evenly in both baskets and insert the baskets in the unit. 4. Select Zone 1, select AIR FRY, set the temperature to 200°C, and set the time to 15 minutes. Select MATCH COOK to match Zone 2 settings to Zone 1. Press the START/PAUSE button to begin cooking. 5. Flip the chicken wings halfway through the cooking time. Sprinkle with sesame seeds if desired. Serve hot.
Per Serving: Calories 467; Fat 17.35g; Sodium 425mg; Carbs 5.99g; Fibre 0.5g; Sugar 3g; Protein 67.27g

Lemon Rosemary Chicken Wings

Prep Time: 15 minutes | Cook Time: 19 minutes | Serves: 2

340 g chicken wings
½ tbsp. olive oil
1 tbsp. soy sauce
1 tsp. fresh ginger, minced
1 tbsp. oyster sauce
3 tbsp. sugar
1 tbsp. fresh rosemary, chopped
½ fresh lemon, cut into wedges

1. Place the chicken wings in a bowl and toss with the oil, soy sauce, and ginger. Refrigerate for 30 minutes. 2. Then place the chicken wings in a baking pan that fits the air fryer basket. Install a crisper plate in the Zone 1 basket. Place the pan in the basket and insert the basket in the unit. 3. Select Zone 1, select AIR FRY, set the temperature to 200°C, and set time for 6 minutes. Press START/PAUSE to begin cooking. 4. Meanwhile, mix together the sugar, rosemary, and oyster sauce in a bowl. 5. When cooking time is up, pour the rosemary mixture over the chicken and top the chicken with the lemon wedges. 6. Continue cooking for an additional 13 minutes, turning the chicken wings halfway through.
Per Serving: Calories 298; Fat 9.54g; Sodium 495mg; Carbs 16.12g; Fibre 0.4g; Sugar 13.59g; Protein 35.36g

Herbed Turkey Breast

Prep time: 60 minutes | Cook time: 55 minutes | Serves: 4

½ teaspoon dried thyme
675g turkey breasts
½ teaspoon dried sage
3 whole star anise
1½ tablespoons olive oil
1½ tablespoons hot mustard
1 teaspoon smoked cayenne pepper
1 teaspoon fine sea salt

1. Brush the turkey breast with olive oil and sprinkle with seasonings. 2. Insert the crisper plate in the basket in zone 1, and transfer the turkey breast to it. 3. Select AIR FRY mode, adjust the cooking temperature to 185°C and set the cooking time to 53 minutes. 4. Press the START/PAUSE button to begin cooking. 5. Spread the cooked breast with the hot mustard after 45 minutes of cooking time. 6. Let the dish rest before slicing and serving.
Per Serving: Calories 304; Fat 9.12g; Sodium 813mg; Carbs 1.47g; Fiber 0.6g; Sugar 0.1g; Protein 51.41g

Lime Chicken Breast with Parsley

Prep time: 30 minutes | Cook time: 26 minutes | Serves: 2

1½ handful fresh parsley, roughly chopped
Fresh juice of ½ lime
1 teaspoon ground black pepper
1 ½ large-sized chicken breasts, cut into halves
1 teaspoon salt
Zest of ½ lime

1. Toss the chicken breasts with the other ingredients and let it marinate a couple of hours. 2. Insert the crisper plate in the basket in zone 1, and transfer the chicken breasts to it. 3. Select ROAST mode, adjust the cooking temperature to 170°C and set the cooking time to 26 minutes. 4. Press the START/PAUSE button to begin cooking. 5. Serve warm.
Per Serving: Calories 374; Fat 8.6g; Sodium 1435mg; Carbs 5.63g; Fiber 1.9g; Sugar 0.76g; Protein 67.05g

Garlic Chicken Sausages

Prep Time: 20 minutes | Cook Time: 15 minutes | Serves: 4

1 garlic clove, diced
1 spring onion, chopped
140 g chicken mince
½ teaspoon salt
½ teaspoon ground black pepper
4 sausages links
1 teaspoon olive oil

1. Combine the chicken mince, onion, diced garlic clove, salt, and ground black pepper in a mixing bowl. 2. Fill the sausage links with the chicken mince mixture. Cut every sausage into halves and secure the endings. 3. Install a crisper plate in both baskets. Brush the sausages with olive oil and place them evenly in the baskets. Then insert the baskets in the unit. 4. Select Zone 1, select AIR FRY, set the temperature to 185°C, and set the time for 10 minutes. Press START/PAUSE to begin cooking. 5. Then flip the sausages on another side and cook for 5 minutes more. Increase the cooking time to 200°C and cook for 8 minutes for faster results.
Per Serving: Calories 573; Fat 40.33g; Sodium 675mg; Carbs 3.52g; Fibre 0.9g; Sugar 0.38g; Protein 47.64g

Spicy Coconut Chicken Strips

Prep Time: 15 minutes | Cook Time: 14 minutes | Serves: 6

900 g chicken breast, skinless, boneless
1 teaspoon salt
1 teaspoon ground turmeric
½ teaspoon cayenne pepper
1 egg, beaten
2 tablespoons coconut flour

1. Cut the chicken breast into the strips and sprinkle with ground turmeric, salt, and cayenne pepper. Then add the beaten egg and whisk well. Then, stir in the coconut flour. 2. Install a crisper plate in both baskets. Place the coated chicken breast evenly in the baskets, then insert the baskets in the unit. 3. Select Zone 1, select AIR FRY, set the temperature to 205°C, and set time to 7 minutes. Select MATCH COOK to match Zone 2 settings to Zone 1. Press the START/PAUSE button to begin cooking. 4. When cooking is complete, serve immediately.
Per Serving: Calories 274; Fat 7.06g; Sodium 522mg; Carbs 0.78g; Fibre 0.2g; Sugar 0.27g; Protein 48.5g

Cheese & Pork Rinds-Crusted Chicken Breast

Prep Time: 15 minutes | Cook Time: 20 minutes | Serves: 6

450 g chicken breast, skinless, boneless
125 g pork rinds
75 g Parmesan, grated
3 eggs, beaten
1 teaspoon chili flakes
1 teaspoon ground paprika
2 tablespoons avocado oil
1 teaspoon Erythritol
¼ teaspoon onion powder
1 teaspoon cayenne pepper
1 chili pepper, minced
½ teaspoon dried dill

1. In a small shallow bowl, mix together the chili flakes, onion powder, ground paprika, Erythritol, and cayenne pepper. Add dried dill and stir the mixture gently. Then rub the chicken breast in the spice mixture and sprinkle with minced chili pepper. 2. Dip the chicken breast in the beaten eggs, then coat it in the Parmesan and dip in the eggs again. Then dredge the chicken in the pork rinds and sprinkle with avocado oil. 3. Install a crisper plate in both baskets. Place the coated chicken evenly in both baskets and insert them in the unit. 4. Select Zone 1, select AIR FRY, set the temperature to 195°C, and set time to 16 minutes. Select MATCH COOK to match Zone 2 settings to Zone 1. Press the START/PAUSE button to begin cooking. 5. Then flip the chicken breast on another side and cook it for an additional 4 minutes.
Per Serving: Calories 362; Fat 20.5g; Sodium 296mg; Carbs 8.09g; Fibre 0.5g; Sugar 1.44g; Protein 34.8g

Savoury Turkey Meatballs with Hoisin Sauce

Prep Time: 15 minutes | Cook Time: 9 minutes | Serves: 4

Meatballs:
590 g 93% lean turkey mince
30 g panko bread crumbs, regular or gluten-free
3 chopped spring onions, plus more for garnish
10 g chopped fresh coriander
1 large egg
1 tablespoon grated fresh ginger
1 garlic clove, minced
1 tablespoon reduced-sodium soy sauce or tamari
2 teaspoons toasted sesame oil
¾ teaspoon salt
Olive oil spray

Hoisin Sauce:
2 tablespoons hoisin sauce
2 tablespoons fresh orange juice
1 tablespoon reduced-sodium soy sauce or tamari

1. Mix together the ground turkey, panko, egg, spring onions, coriander, garlic, ginger, soy sauce, sesame oil, and salt in a large bowl. Then roll the mixture into 12 meatballs and spritz with olive oil. 2. Install a crisper plate in both baskets. Place the meatballs in a single layer in both baskets. Then insert the baskets in unit. 3. Select Zone 1, select AIR FRY, set the temperature to 195°C, and set time to 9 minutes. Select MATCH COOK to match Zone 2 settings to Zone 1. Press the START/PAUSE button to begin cooking. 4. Flip halfway through the cooking time. Cook until the centre is brown. 5. In the meantime, mix up the orange juice, hoisin sauce, and soy sauce in a saucepan and bring to a boil over medium-low heat. Reduce the heat to low and cook until the sauce is reduced slightly, 2 to 3 minutes. 6. Drizzle the meatballs with the sauce and serve topped with spring onions.

Per Serving: Calories 309; Fat 17.49g; Sodium 1188mg; Carbs 7.54g; Fibre 0.7g; Sugar 3.43g; Protein 30.68g

Crispy Chicken Cutlets with Lemon-Caper Sauce

Prep Time: 15 minutes | Cook Time: 6 minutes | Serves: 4

Chicken:
2 (200 g) boneless, skinless chicken breasts, all fat trimmed
¼ teaspoon salt
Freshly ground black pepper
2 large egg whites
65 g seasoned bread crumbs, whole wheat or gluten-free
Olive oil spray
Sauce:
1 tablespoon whipped butter
120 ml reduced-sodium chicken stock
60 ml dry white wine
Juice of 1 lemon, lemon halves reserved
Freshly ground black pepper
1 tablespoon capers, drained
For Serving:
1 lemon, sliced
Chopped fresh parsley leaves

1. Cut the chicken breasts in half horizontally and cut a total of 4 pieces. Place the chicken breasts between two sheets of parchment paper. Pound them to ½ cm thickness with a heavy pan or meat mallet. Season both sides with salt and pepper. 2. In a shallow bowl, whisk the egg whites with 1 teaspoon water. Place the bread crumbs on a large plate. Dip each piece of chicken in the egg, then dredge in the bread crumbs. Shake off any excess and place them on a work surface. Generously spray both sides of the chicken with olive oil. 3. Install a crisper plate in both baskets. Place the chicken cutlets in a single layer in both baskets. Then insert the baskets in unit. 4. Select Zone 1, select AIR FRY, set the temperature to 185°C, and set time to 6 minutes. Select MATCH COOK to match Zone 2 settings to Zone 1. Press the START/PAUSE button to begin cooking. 5. Flip halfway through the cooking time. Cook until crisp and golden. 6. In the meantime, melt the butter in a medium frying pan over medium heat. Add the chicken broth, wine, reserved lemon halves, lemon juice, and pepper to taste. 7. Boil over high heat until the liquid is reduced by half, 3 to 4 minutes. Remove from the heat. Discard the lemon halves and stir in the capers. 8. Divide the chicken among serving plates. Spoon 2 tablespoons of the sauce over each piece of chicken. Top with the lemon slices and parsley and serve.
Per Serving: Calories 294; Fat 12.55g; Sodium 705mg; Carbs 30.2g; Fibre 2.6g; Sugar 7.35g; Protein 15.58g

Cornflake-Crusted Chicken Drumsticks

Prep Time: 15 minutes | Cook Time: 28 minutes | Serves: 4

Chicken:
8 bone-in chicken drumsticks, skin removed
½ teaspoon salt
2 large eggs
½ teaspoon sweet paprika
¼ teaspoon garlic powder
¼ teaspoon chili powder
Olive oil spray

Crumb Coating:
80 g regular or gluten-free cornflakes
Olive oil spray
1 teaspoon salt
1 tablespoon dried parsley
1½ teaspoons sweet paprika
1 teaspoon dried marjoram
1 teaspoon dried thyme
½ teaspoon garlic powder
½ teaspoon onion powder
¼ teaspoon chili powder

For the chicken: Sprinkle the chicken with salt. Whisk the eggs with 1 teaspoon water, garlic powder, paprika, and chili powder in a shallow bowl and set aside.

For the crumb coating: 1. Place the nachos in a gallon zip-top bag and crush with a rolling pin to keep the flakes in shape. 2. Transfer to a shallow bowl. Sprinkle a little oil on the cornflakes and add the salt, paprika, marjoram, parsley, thyme, onion powder, garlic powder, and paprika. Stir well to combine. 3. Dip each drumstick in the egg mix, then dredge in the crumbs. Transfer to a work surface and spray with oil on all sides. 4. Install a crisper plate in both baskets. Place the chicken in a single layer in both baskets. Then insert the baskets in unit. 5. Select Zone 1, select AIR FRY, set the temperature to 175°C, and set time to 28 minutes. Select MATCH COOK to match Zone 2 settings to Zone 1. Press the START/PAUSE button to begin cooking. 6. Flip halfway through the cooking time. Cook until the chicken is cooked through and the coating is golden. Let cool for 5 minutes before serving.

Per Serving: Calories 444; Fat 24.59g; Sodium 1190mg; Carbs 12.54g; Fibre 1.1g; Sugar 0.71g; Protein 41.17g

Chapter 4 Red Meat

Spicy Garlic Steak 33

Roasted London Broil with Herb Butter 33

Delicious Hawaiian Butter Beef Rolls 34

Meatballs with Tomato Sauce 34

Cajun Beef Tenderloins 35

Filet Mignon Steaks with Cream-Garlic Sauce 35

Whisky Sirloin Steak 36

Cheese Pork Stuffed Peppers 36

Herbed Garlic Porterhouse Steak 37

Savoury Beef Hamburgers 37

Air Fried Butter Beef Steak 38

Delicious Beef Meatloaves 38

Crispy Bacon Slices 39

Flank Steak with Potatoes 39

Spicy Garlic Steak

Prep time: 20 minutes | Cook time: 15 minutes | Serves: 2

½ Ancho chili pepper, soaked in hot water before using
1 tablespoon brandy
2 teaspoons smoked paprika
1 ½ tablespoons olive oil
2 beef steaks
Salt, to taste
1 teaspoon ground allspice
3 cloves garlic, sliced

1. Sprinkle the beef steaks with salt, paprika, and allspice. Scatter the sliced garlic over the top. 2. Drizzle the steak with brandy and olive oil; spread minced Ancho chili pepper over the top. 3. Insert the crisper plate in the basket in zone 1, and transfer the food to it. 4. Select BAKE mode, adjust the cooking temperature to 195°C and set the cooking time to 14 minutes. 5. Press the START/PAUSE button to begin cooking. 6. Flip the steaks halfway through cooking. 7. Serve warm.
Per Serving: Calories 444; Fat 23.74g; Sodium 490mg; Carbs 5.68g; Fiber 2g; Sugar 0.36g; Protein 50.44g

Roasted London Broil with Herb Butter

Prep Time: 10 minutes | Cook Time: 28 minutes | Serves: 4

455 g London broil
60 ml freshly squeezed lemon juice
60 ml olive oil
2 tablespoons tamari sauce
1 tablespoon stone-ground mustard
1 teaspoon mixed peppercorns, whole
3 tablespoons butter, cold
2 tablespoons fresh Italian herbs
1 teaspoon garlic powder
½ teaspoon salt

1. Toss the beef with the olive oil, lemon juice, mustard, tamari sauce, and peppercorns and let marinate for an hour. 2. Install a crisper plate in the Zone 1 basket, place the beef in a lightly oiled basket, and discard the marinade. 3. Insert the basket into the unit. The unit will default to Zone 1. Select AIR FRY. Set the temperature to 205°C and set the time to 28 minutes. Press the START/PAUSE button to begin cooking. Press the START/PAUSE button to turn it over halfway through the cooking time. 4. Meanwhile, mix the butter, herbs, garlic powder with salt. 5. When the cooking is complete, serve warm beef with the chilled herb butter on the side. Bon appétit!
Per Serving: Calories 444; Fat 32.97g; Sodium 471mg; Carbs 2.78g; Fibre 0.5g; Sugar 0.9g; Protein 35.6g

Delicious Hawaiian Butter Beef Rolls

Prep Time: 10 minutes | Cook Time: 15 minutes | Serves: 4

455 g beef, minced
100 g seasoned breadcrumbs
1 tablespoon fresh coriander, finely chopped
1 tablespoon fresh parsley, finely chopped
8 Hawaiian butter dinner rolls

1. Mix all ingredients, except for the rolls. Shape the mixture into four patties. 2. Install a crisper plate in the Zone 1 basket, place the patties in the basket, and insert the basket into the unit. The unit will default to Zone 1. Select AIR FRY. Set the temperature to 195°C and set the time to 15 minutes. Press the START/PAUSE button to begin cooking until cooked through. Press the START/PAUSE button to turn it over halfway through the cooking time. 3. When the cooking is complete, serve the burgers on the prepared rolls and enjoy!

Per Serving: Calories 414; Fat 10.01g; Sodium 2855mg; Carbs 45.67g; Fibre 6.7g; Sugar 4.63g; Protein 29.66g

Meatballs with Tomato Sauce

Prep time: 20 minutes | Cook time: 15 minutes | Serves: 4

For the Meatballs:
4 tablespoons parmesan, grated
60g green onion
455g beef sausage meat
3 garlic cloves, minced
⅓ teaspoon ground black pepper
Sea salt, to taste
For the Sauce:
2 tablespoons Worcestershire sauce
⅓ yellow onion, minced
Dash of Tabasco sauce
60g tomato paste
1 teaspoon cumin powder
½ tablespoon balsamic vinegar

1. Knead all of the meatball ingredients until everything is well incorporated. 2. Roll the mixture into balls. 3. Insert the crisper plate in the basket in zone 1, and transfer the meatballs to it. 4. Select AIR FRY mode, adjust the cooking temperature to 185°C and set the cooking time to 13 minutes. 5. Press the START/PAUSE button to begin cooking. 6. In a saucepan, cook the ingredients for the sauce until thoroughly warmed. 7. Serve the meatballs with the tomato sauce.

Per Serving: Calories 364; Fat 27.21g; Sodium 515mg; Carbs 9g; Fiber 0.7g; Sugar 3.58g; Protein 19.88g

Cajun Beef Tenderloins

Prep time: 1 hour 5 minutes | Cook time: 25 minutes | Serves: 2

80ml beef stock
2 tablespoons Cajun seasoning, crushed
½ teaspoon garlic powder
340g beef tenderloins
½ tablespoon pear cider vinegar
⅓ teaspoon cayenne pepper
1 ½ tablespoon olive oil
½ teaspoon freshly ground black pepper
1 teaspoon salt

1. Coat the beef tenderloins with salt, cayenne pepper, and black pepper. 2. Mix the remaining items in a medium-sized bowl; let the meat marinate for 40 minutes in this mixture. 3. Transfer the food to the basket in zone 1. 4. Select ROAST mode, adjust the cooking temperature to 195°C and set the cooking time to 22 minutes. 5. Press the START/PAUSE button to begin cooking. 6. Flip the food halfway through cooking. 7. Serve warm.
Per Serving: Calories 489; Fat 25.42g; Sodium 1657mg; Carbs 7.38g; Fiber 1.5g; Sugar 1.83g; Protein 53.27g

Filet Mignon Steaks with Cream-Garlic Sauce

Prep time: 25 minutes | Cook time: 25 minutes | Serves: 6

40g butter, at room temperature
120g heavy cream
½ medium-sized garlic bulb, peeled and pressed
6 filet mignon steaks
2 teaspoons mixed peppercorns, freshly cracked
1 ½ tablespoons apple cider
A dash of hot sauce
1½ teaspoons sea salt flakes

1. Season the mignon steaks with the cracked peppercorns and salt flakes. 2. Insert the crisper plates in the baskets. 3. Divide the mignon steaks between the baskets in zone 1 and zone 2. 4. Select ROAST mode, adjust the cooking temperature to 195°C and set the cooking time to 24 minutes. 5. Press the MATCH COOK button and copy the zone 1 settings to zone 2. 6. Press the START/PAUSE button to begin cooking. 7. Flip the steaks halfway through cooking. 8. In a small nonstick saucepan that is placed over a moderate flame, mash the garlic to a smooth paste. Whisk in the rest of the above ingredients. Whisk constantly until it has a uniform consistency. 9. Lay the filet mignon steaks on serving plates; spoon a little sauce onto each filet mignon. Enjoy.
Per Serving: Calories 435; Fat 35.78g; Sodium 726mg; Carbs 2.75g; Fiber 0.7g; Sugar 1.86g; Protein 24.81g

Whisky Sirloin Steak

Prep time: 25 minutes | Cook time: 25 minutes | Serves: 6

900g sirloin steaks
1½ tablespoons tamari sauce
⅓ teaspoon cayenne pepper
⅓ teaspoon ground ginger
2 garlic cloves, thinly sliced
2 tablespoons Irish whiskey
2 tablespoons olive oil
Fine sea salt, to taste

1. Add all the ingredients, minus the olive oil and the steak, to a resealable plastic bag. 2. Throw in the steak and let it marinate for a couple of hours. After that, drizzle the sirloin steaks with 2 tablespoons olive oil. 3. Insert the crisper plates in the baskets. Divide the steaks between the baskets in zone 1 and zone 2. 4. Select ROAST mode, adjust the cooking temperature to 200°C and set the cooking time to 22 minutes. 5. Press the MATCH COOK button and copy the zone 1 settings to zone 2. 6. Press the START/PAUSE button to begin cooking. 7. Flip the steals halfway through cooking. 8. Serve warm.
Per Serving: Calories 214; Fat 8.42g; Sodium 571mg; Carbs 1.87g; Fiber 0.1g; Sugar 1.26g; Protein 30.86g

Cheese Pork Stuffed Peppers

Prep time: 30 minutes | Cook time: 25 minutes | Serves: 3

3 peppers, stems and seeds removed
1 tablespoon rapeseed oil
80g onions, chopped
1 teaspoon fresh garlic, minced
1 Mexican chili pepper, finely chopped
455g lean pork, minced
½ teaspoon sea salt
½ teaspoon black pepper
1 tablespoon Mexican oregano
1 ripe tomato, pureed
75g cheese, grated

1. Cook the peppers in boiling salted water for 4 minutes. 2. In a nonstick frying pan, heat the rapeseed oil over medium heat. Then, sauté the onions, garlic and Mexican chili pepper until tender and fragrant. 3. Stir in the pork mince and continue sautéing until the pork has browned; drain off the excess fat. 4. Stir in the salt, black pepper, Mexican oregano, and pureed tomato. 5. Divide the filling among the peppers. 6. Insert the crisper plate in the basket in zone 1, and transfer the stuffed peppers to it. 7. Select BAKE mode, adjust the cooking temperature to 190°C and set the cooking time to 19 minutes. 8. Press the START/PAUSE button to begin cooking. 9. Top the peppers with grated feta cheese after 13 minutes of cooking time. 10. Serve warm.
Per Serving: Calories 350; Fat 19.09g; Sodium 2558mg; Carbs 14.73g; Fibre 2.1g; Sugar 9.21g; Protein 32.39g

Herbed Garlic Porterhouse Steak

Prep Time: 10 minutes | Cook Time: 12 minutes | Serves: 4

675 g Porterhouse steak
1 tablespoon olive oil
Salt and ground black pepper, to taste
½ teaspoon cayenne pepper
1 teaspoon dried parsley
1 teaspoon dried oregano
½ teaspoon dried basil
2 tablespoons butter
2 garlic cloves, minced

1. Place the steak in a large bowl and toss with the remaining ingredients. 2. Install a crisper plate in the Zone 1 basket. Place the steak in the basket and insert it in the unit. 3. Select Zone 1, select AIR FRY, set the temperature to 205°C, and set the time for 12 minutes. Press START/PAUSE to begin cooking. 4. Flipping halfway through the cooking time. Enjoy!

Per Serving: Calories 460; Fat 34.02g; Sodium 136mg; Carbs 1.93g; Fibre 0.4g; Sugar 0.63g; Protein 35.1g

Savoury Beef Hamburgers

Prep Time: 15 minutes | Cook Time: 15 minutes | Serves: 3

375 g beef mince
2 cloves garlic, minced
1 small onion, chopped
Salt and ground black pepper, to taste
3 hamburger buns

1. In a mixing bowl, toss the beef with the remaining ingredients until well combined. Form the mixture into three patties. 2. Install a crisper plate in the Zone 1 basket. Place the patties in the basket and insert it in the unit. 3. Select Zone 1, select AIR FRY, set the temperature to 195°C, and set the time for 15 minutes. Press START/PAUSE to begin cooking. 4. Flipping halfway through the cooking time. 5. Enjoy in hamburger buns!

Per Serving: Calories 423; Fat 19.98g; Sodium 288mg; Carbs 25.32g; Fibre 1.5g; Sugar 4.45g; Protein 33.46g

Chapter 4 Red Meat

Air Fried Butter Beef Steak

Prep Time: 5 minutes | Cook Time: 10 minutes | Serves: 2

1 tablespoon steak rub
1 teaspoon liquid smoke
1 tablespoon low-salt soy sauce
200g steaks
melted butter
salt & pepper, to taste

1. Drizzle the steaks with the liquid smoke and soy sauce, massage well until incorporated. Then season the steak with the steak rub. 2. Place the seasoned steak in the refrigerator to marinate for about 2 hours. 3. Install a crisper plate in the Zone 1 basket. Place the marinated steak in the basket and insert it in the unit. 4. Select Zone 1, select AIR FRY, set the temperature to 190°C, and set the time for 5 minutes. Press START/PAUSE to begin cooking. 5. Check the steak for desired doneness then cook for extra minutes if desired until tender and crispy to taste. 6. Serve, drizzled with the melted butter and season with salt and pepper to taste.

Per Serving: Calories 302; Fat 17.37g; Sodium 946mg; Carbs 4.5g; Fibre 0.6g; Sugar 2.48g; Protein 32.7g

Delicious Beef Meatloaves

Prep Time: 10 minutes | Cook Time: 10 minutes | Serves: 10

60 g ketchup
35 g diced onion
30 g coconut flour
½ teaspoon sea salt
½ teaspoon black pepper
½ teaspoon dried tarragon
50 g blanched almond flour
455 g beef mince
1 minced garlic clove
1 teaspoon Italian seasoning
1 tablespoon Worcestershire sauce
2 beaten eggs

1. Combine all ingredients in a large mixing bowl and incorporate until a batter is formed. 2. Mold 10 even loaves from the batter then place in the refrigerator to firm up for about 15 minutes. 3. Install a crisper plate in both baskets. Transfer the firm loaves into the fryer baskets and inserts basket in the unit. 4. Select Zone 1, select AIR FRY, set the temperature to 180°C, and set time to 10 minutes. Select MATCH COOK to match Zone 2 settings to Zone 1. Press the START/PAUSE button to begin cooking. 5. Serve hot.

Per Serving: Calories 177; Fat 10.8g; Sodium 264mg; Carbs 4.4g; Fibre 0.9g; Sugar 2.23g; Protein 15.61g

Crispy Bacon Slices

Prep Time: 4 minutes | Cook Time: 10 minutes | Serves: 10

10 bacon slices
beef seasoning

1. Generously rub the bacon slices with the seasonings. 2. Install a crisper plate in the Zone 1 basket. Place the seasoned bacon slices in the basket and insert it in the unit. 3. Select Zone 1, select AIR FRY, set the temperature to 205°C, and set the time for 10 minutes. Press START/PAUSE to begin cooking. 4. Cook until crisp. Serve and enjoy as desired.
Per Serving: Calories 107; Fat 10.21g; Sodium 143mg; Carbs 0.38g; Fibre 0g; Sugar 0.25g; Protein 3.27g

Flank Steak with Potatoes

Prep Time: 15 minutes | Cook Time: 20 minutes | Serves: 2

455 g extra-small Red Bliss potatoes, unpeeled
3 tablespoons extra-virgin olive oil
Salt and pepper
2 teaspoons honey, warmed
1 (300 g) flank steak, trimmed and halved with grain
2 tablespoons minced fresh parsley
1½ teaspoons red wine vinegar
1½ teaspoons minced fresh oregano or ½ teaspoon dried
1 garlic clove, minced
⅛ teaspoon red pepper flakes

1. In a mixing bowl, toss the red potatoes with 2 teaspoons oil, ¼ teaspoon salt and ¼ teaspoon pepper. 2. Install a crisper plate in the Zone 1 basket. Transfer the potatoes to the basket and insert the basket into the unit. 3. Select Zone 1, select AIR FRY, set the temperature to 205°C, and set the time for 12 minutes. Press START/PAUSE to begin cooking. 4. Meanwhile, mix up the honey and 1 teaspoon oil in a small bowl. Pat dry the steaks with paper towels and brush with honey-oil mixture. Then season with salt and pepper to taste. 5. Place the steaks on top of the potatoes, spaced evenly apart. Cook until steaks are browned, about 8 to 10 minutes. flipping the steaks halfway through the cooking process. Transfer steaks to cutting board and place the potatoes in a serving bowl. Tent each with aluminum foil and set aside. 6. In a bowl, combine the remaining 2 tablespoons oil, oregano, parsley, garlic, vinegar, and pepper flakes. Season with salt and pepper to taste. Slice the steaks thin against grain and serve with potatoes and chimichurri.
Per Serving: Calories 397; Fat 13.79g; Sodium 357mg; Carbs 45.64g; Fibre 4.8g; Sugar 10.55g; Protein 23.6g

Chapter 5 Fish and Seafood

Tasty Crab & Cauliflower Cakes ………………………………………… 41

Lemony Salmon with Chives ……………………………………………… 41

Crispy Cod Fillets ………………………………………………………… 42

Crab Cakes with Capers …………………………………………………… 42

Lemon Salmon Steaks……………………………………………………… 43

Crispy Fish Fillets ………………………………………………………… 43

Crunchy Breaded Prawn …………………………………………………… 44

Crispy Fish Sticks ………………………………………………………… 44

Tasty Air Fryer Sea Bream ………………………………………………… 45

Breaded Crab Croquettes ………………………………………………… 45

Crispy Prawns Scampi …………………………………………………… 46

Delicious Honey Glazed Halibut Steaks ………………………………… 46

Simple Air Fryer Tilapia ………………………………………………… 47

Crispy Breaded Prawns with Cocktail Sauce …………………………… 47

Lemony Sea bass ………………………………………………………… 48

Garlic Prawns with Alfredo Pasta ……………………………………… 48

Crunchy Haddock Sticks…………………………………………………… 49

Tasty Crab & Cauliflower Cakes

Prep time: 20 minutes | Cook time: 12 minutes | Serves: 4

1½ tablespoons mayonnaise
½ teaspoon whole-grain mustard
2 eggs, well beaten
⅓ teaspoon ground black pepper
225g smashed cauliflower
½ teaspoon dried dill weed
225g crabmeat
A pinch of salt
1½ tablespoons softened butter

1. Mix all the ingredients thoroughly. Shape the mixture into 4 patties. 2. Insert the crisper plate in the basket in zone 1, and transfer the chicken thighs to it. 3. Select AIR FRY mode, adjust the cooking temperature to 185°C and set the cooking time to 12 minutes. 4. Press the START/PAUSE button to begin cooking. 5. Flip the patties halfway through cooking. 6. Serve the patties over boiled potatoes.
Per Serving: Calories 148; Fat 8.21g; Sodium 544mg; Carbs 4.48g; Fiber 1.2g; Sugar 1.57g; Protein 14.21g

Lemony Salmon with Chives

Prep time: 50 minutes | Cook time: 10 minutes | Serves: 4

675g salmon steak
½ teaspoon grated lemon zest
Freshly cracked mixed peppercorns, to taste
80ml lemon juice
Fresh chopped chives, for garnish
120ml dry white wine
½ teaspoon fresh coriander, chopped
Fine sea salt, to taste

1. Place all ingredients, except for salmon steak and chives, in a deep pan. Bring to a boil over medium-high flame until it has reduced by half. Allow it to cool down. 2. Allow the salmon steak to marinate in the lemon sauce in refrigerator for about 40 minutes. 3. Insert the crisper plate in the basket in zone 1, and transfer the salmon steak to it. 4. Select AIR FRY mode, adjust the cooking temperature to 205°C and set the cooking time to 10 minutes. 5. Press the START/PAUSE button to begin cooking. 6. Brush the salmon steak with the reserved marinade and garnish with fresh chopped chives.
Per Serving: Calories 471; Fat 14.41g; Sodium 888mg; Carbs 66.61g; Fiber 2.9g; Sugar 24.53g; Protein 38.33g

Crispy Cod Fillets

Prep time: 20 minutes | Cook time: 10 minutes | Serves: 2

2 medium-sized cod fillets
½ tablespoon fresh lemon juice
1 ½ tablespoons olive oil
½ tablespoon whole-grain mustard
Sea salt and ground black pepper, to savor
60g coconut flour
2 eggs

1. Thoroughly combine olive oil and coconut flour in a shallow bowl. 2. In another shallow bowl, whisk the egg. 3. Drizzle each cod fillet with lemon juice and spread with mustard. Sprinkle each fillet with salt and ground black pepper. 4. Dip each fish fillet into the whisked egg; now, roll each of them in the olive oil/coconut flour mix. 5. Insert the crisper plates in the baskets. Divide the cod fillets between the baskets in zone 1 and zone 2. 6. Select AIR FRY mode, adjust the cooking temperature to 180°C and set the cooking time to 10 minutes. 7. Press the MATCH COOK button and copy the zone 1 settings to zone 2. 8. Press the START/PAUSE button to begin cooking. 9. Flip the cod fillets halfway through cooking. 10. Serve the dish with potato salad.
Per Serving: Calories 255; Fat 14.97g; Sodium 447mg; Carbs 5.19g; Fiber 0.9g; Sugar 2.2g; Protein 24.17g

Crab Cakes with Capers

Prep time: 20 minutes | Cook time: 12 minutes | Serves: 5

⅓ teaspoon ground black pepper
½ tablespoon nonpareil capers
3 eggs, well whisked
½ teaspoon dried dill weed
1½ tablespoons softened butter
½ teaspoon whole-grain mustard
225g crabmeat
100g Romano cheese, grated
2½ tablespoons mayonnaise
A pinch of salt

1. Mix all the ingredients thoroughly. 2. Shape the mixture into 4 balls and press each ball to form the cakes. 3. Spritz your cakes with cooking oil. 4. Insert the crisper plates in the baskets. Divide the cakes between the baskets in zone 1 and zone 2. 5. Select BAKE mode, adjust the cooking temperature to 185°C and set the cooking time to 12 minutes. 6. Press the MATCH COOK button and copy the zone 1 settings to zone 2. 7. Press the START/PAUSE button to begin cooking. 8. Flip the cakes halfway through cooking. 9. Serve warm.
Per Serving: Calories 204; Fat 13.21g; Sodium 605mg; Carbs 2.62g; Fiber 0.1g; Sugar 0.7g; Protein 17.99g

Lemon Salmon Steaks

Prep time: 20 minutes | Cook time: 12 minutes | Serves: 2

2 salmon steaks
Coarse sea salt, to taste
¼ teaspoon freshly ground black pepper, or more to taste
1 tablespoon sesame oil
Zest of 1 lemon
1 tablespoon fresh lemon juice
1 teaspoon garlic, minced
½ teaspoon smoked cayenne pepper
½ teaspoon dried dill

1. Pat dry the salmon steaks with a kitchen towel. 2. In a ceramic dish, combine the remaining ingredients until everything is well whisked. 3. Add the salmon steaks to the ceramic dish and let them sit in the refrigerator for 1 hour. 4. Insert the crisper plate in the basket in zone 1, and transfer the salmon steaks to it. 5. Select AIR FRY mode, adjust the cooking temperature to 190°C and set the cooking time to 12 minutes. 6. Press the START/PAUSE button to begin cooking. 7. Flip the salmon steaks halfway through cooking. 8. Cook the marinade in a small sauté pan over a moderate flame until the sauce has thickened. 9. Pour the sauce over the steaks and serve.
Per Serving: Calories 547; Fat 21.97g; Sodium 276mg; Carbs 3.2g; Fibre 0.4g; Sugar 0.86g; Protein 80.1g

Crispy Fish Fillets

Prep Time: 10 minutes | Cook Time: 5 minutes | Serves: 4

2 fish fillets, each sliced into 4 pieces
1 tbsp. lemon juice
1 tsp. chili powder
4 tbsp. mayonnaise
3 tbsp. semolina
¼ tsp. black pepper
4 tbsp. flour
¼ tsp. salt

1. In a bowl, mix together the flour, semolina, salt, pepper, and chili powder. 2. In a shallow bowl, mix up the lemon juice and mayonnaise. 3. Coat the fillets in the mayonnaise mixture, then dredge in the flour mixture. 4. Install a crisper plate in the Zone 1 basket. Place the coated fish in the basket and insert the basket into the unit. 5. Select Zone 1, select AIR FRY, set the temperature to 205°C, and set the time for 5 minutes. Press START/PAUSE to begin cooking. 6. Once done, serve hot.
Per Serving: Calories 199; Fat 10.39g; Sodium 318mg; Carbs 12.96g; Fibre 1g; Sugar 0.41g; Protein 12.69g

Crunchy Breaded Prawn

Prep Time: 15 minutes | Cook Time: 8 minutes | Serves: 8

900 g prawn, peeled and deveined
4 egg whites
2 tbsp. olive oil
120 g flour
½ tsp. cayenne pepper
100 g bread crumbs
Salt and pepper to taste

1. In a shallow bowl, mix together the flour, pepper, and salt. 2. In a separate bowl, whisk in the egg whites. 3. In a third bowl, mix up the bread crumbs, salt and cayenne pepper. 4. Coat the prawn with the flour mixture, then dip in the egg white and finally rolling in the bread crumbs. 5. Install a crisper plate in the Zone 1 basket. Place the coated prawn in the basket and top with a light drizzle of olive oil. Then insert the basket into the unit. 6. Select Zone 1, select AIR FRY, set the temperature to 205°C, and set the time for 8 minutes. Press START/PAUSE to begin cooking. (If one basket can't fit so much food, you can choose to cook with the Zone 2 basket and use the MATCH COOK mode) 7. When cooking is complete, serve immediately.

Per Serving: Calories 206; Fat 4.31g; Sodium 185mg; Carbs 14.8g; Fibre 0.7g; Sugar 0.71g; Protein 26.72g

Crispy Fish Sticks

Prep Time: 10 minutes | Cook Time: 10 minutes | Serves: 4

455 g tilapia fillets, cut into strips
1 large egg, beaten
2 tsp. Old Bay seasoning
1 tbsp. olive oil
100 g bread crumbs

1. Mix together the bread crumbs, Old Bay, and oil in a shallow bowl. Whisk the egg in a small bowl. 2. Dredge the fish sticks in the egg and then coat them with bread crumbs. 3. Install a crisper plate in the Zone 1 basket. Place the fish in the basket and insert the basket into the unit. 4. Select Zone 1, select AIR FRY, set the temperature to 205°C, and set the time for 10 minutes. Press START/PAUSE to begin cooking. 5. Once done, serve hot.

Per Serving: Calories 177; Fat 6.75g; Sodium 104mg; Carbs 4.7g; Fibre 0.3g; Sugar 0.52g; Protein 24.24g

Tasty Air Fryer Sea Bream

Prep Time: 15 minutes | Cook Time: 10 minutes | Serves: 3

455 g sea bream steaks (pieces)
1 egg, beaten
1 tablespoon coconut flour
1 teaspoon garlic powder
1 tablespoon almond butter, melted
½ teaspoon Erythritol
½ teaspoon chili powder
1 teaspoon apple cider vinegar

1. Mix up the garlic powder, chili powder, coconut flour, and Erythritol in the shallow bowl. Season the sea bream steaks with apple cider vinegar and dip in the beaten egg. After this, coat every fish steak in the coconut flour mixture. 2. Install a crisper plate in the Zone 1 basket, place the fish steak in the basket in one layer and sprinkle with almond butter. Insert the basket into the unit. The unit will default to Zone 1. Select AIR FRY. Set the temperature to 200°C and set the time to 5 minutes. Press the START/PAUSE button to begin cooking. Cook them for 5 minutes from each side. 3. Press the START/PAUSE button to turn the bream steaks and cook for another 15 minutes. 4. When the cooking is complete, remove and serve.
Per Serving: Calories 292; Fat 14.7g; Sodium 217mg; Carbs 1.96g; Fibre 0.3g; Sugar 0.84g; Protein 37.92g

Breaded Crab Croquettes

Prep Time: 15 minutes | Cook Time: 18 minutes | Serves: 6

455 g crab meat
100 g bread crumbs
2 egg whites
½ tsp. parsley
¼ tsp. chives
¼ tsp. tarragon
2 tbsp. celery, chopped
35 g red pepper, chopped
1 tsp. olive oil
½ tsp. lime juice
4 tbsp. sour cream
4 tbsp. mayonnaise
35 g onion, chopped
¼ tsp. salt

1. Combine the bread crumbs and salt in a shallow bowl. 2. Whisk the egg whites in another bowl. 3. In a third bowl, mix up the remaining ingredients and shape equal amounts of the mixture into small balls with your hands and dip each ball in the egg white. Then coat with the bread crumbs. 4. Install a crisper plate in the Zone 1 basket. Place the croquettes in the basket and insert the basket into the unit. 5. Select Zone 1, select AIR FRY, set the temperature to 205°C, and set the time for 18 minutes. Press START/PAUSE to begin cooking. 6. Once done, serve hot.
Per Serving: Calories 311; Fat 7.26g; Sodium 238mg; Carbs 33.62g; Fibre 13.7g; Sugar 0.92g; Protein 31.52g

Crispy Prawns Scampi

Prep time: 20 minutes | Cook time: 10 minutes | Serves: 4

2 egg whites
60g coconut flour
100g Parmigiano-Reggiano, grated
½ teaspoon celery seeds
½ teaspoon porcini powder
½ teaspoon onion powder
1 teaspoon garlic powder
½ teaspoon dried rosemary
½ teaspoon sea salt
½ teaspoon ground black pepper
675g prawns, deveined

1. Whisk the egg with coconut flour and Parmigiano-Reggiano. Add in seasonings and mix to combine well. 2. Dip your prawns in the batter. Roll until they are covered on all sides. 3. Insert the crisper plates in the baskets. Divide the prawns between the baskets in zone 1 and zone 2. 4. Select ROAST mode, adjust the cooking temperature to 200°C and set the cooking time to 7 minutes. 5. Press the MATCH COOK button and copy the zone 1 settings to zone 2. 6. Press the START/PAUSE button to begin cooking. 7. Serve the dish with lemon wedges if desired.
Per Serving: Calories 296; Fat 9.45g; Sodium 2282mg; Carbs 6.17g; Fibre 0.6g; Sugar 1.25g; Protein 44.17g

Delicious Honey Glazed Halibut Steaks

Prep Time: 15 minutes | Cook Time: 10 minutes | Serves: 4

455 g halibut steaks
Salt and pepper to taste
1 tsp. dried basil
2 tbsp. honey
60 ml vegetable oil
2½ tbsp. Worcester sauce
1 tbsp. freshly squeezed lemon juice
2 tbsp. vermouth
1 tbsp. fresh parsley leaves, coarsely chopped

1. In a large bowl, toss the fish with the remaining ingredients until well coated. 2. Install a crisper plate in the Zone 1 basket. Place the coated fish in the basket and insert it in the unit. 3. Select Zone 1, select AIR FRY, set the temperature to 200°C, and set the time for 5 minutes. Press START/PAUSE to begin cooking. 4. When cooking is complete, turn the fish over and allow to cook for another 5 minutes. 5. Serve with a side of potato salad.
Per Serving: Calories 381; Fat 29.38g; Sodium 173mg; Carbs 11.89g; Fibre 0.5g; Sugar 10.32g; Protein 16.82g

Simple Air Fryer Tilapia

Prep Time: 5 minutes | Cook Time: 7 minutes | Serves: 4

455 g tilapia fillets
½ tsp. lemon pepper
Salt to taste

1. Install a crisper plate in the Zone 1 basket and grease with cooking spray. Place the tilapia fillets in the basket and sprinkle with the lemon pepper and salt. Then insert the basket into the unit. 2. Select Zone 1, select AIR FRY, set the temperature to 205°C, and set the time for 7 minutes. Press START/PAUSE to begin cooking. 3. Serve with a side of vegetables.
Per Serving: Calories 110; Fat 1.97g; Sodium 204mg; Carbs 0.13g; Fibre 0.1g; Sugar 0.02g; Protein 22.8g

Crispy Breaded Prawns with Cocktail Sauce

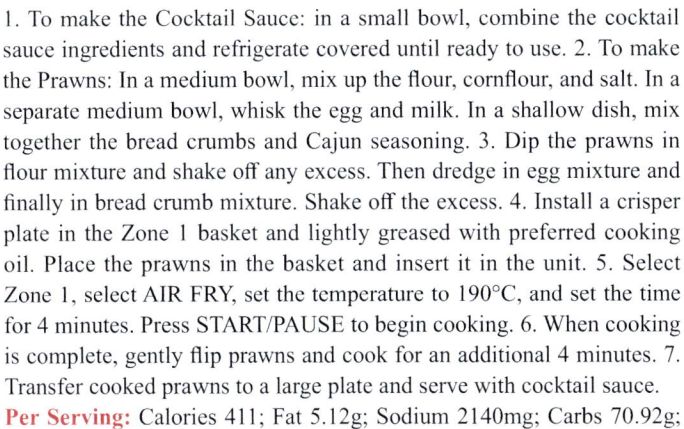

Prep Time: 10 minutes | Cook Time: 8 minutes | Serves: 2

For Cocktail Sauce:
240 g ketchup
2 tablespoons prepared horseradish
1 tablespoon lemon juice
½ teaspoon Worcestershire sauce
⅛ teaspoon Tabasco sauce
⅛ teaspoon chili powder
¼ teaspoon salt
⅛ teaspoon ground black pepper

For Prawns:
40 g gluten-free flour
2 tablespoons cornflour
1 teaspoon salt
60 ml whole milk
1 large egg
55 g gluten-free plain panko bread crumbs
1 tablespoon Cajun seasoning
225 g medium raw prawns, tail on, deveined and shelled

1. To make the Cocktail Sauce: in a small bowl, combine the cocktail sauce ingredients and refrigerate covered until ready to use. 2. To make the Prawns: In a medium bowl, mix up the flour, cornflour, and salt. In a separate medium bowl, whisk the egg and milk. In a shallow dish, mix together the bread crumbs and Cajun seasoning. 3. Dip the prawns in flour mixture and shake off any excess. Then dredge in egg mixture and finally in bread crumb mixture. Shake off the excess. 4. Install a crisper plate in the Zone 1 basket and lightly greased with preferred cooking oil. Place the prawns in the basket and insert it in the unit. 5. Select Zone 1, select AIR FRY, set the temperature to 190°C, and set the time for 4 minutes. Press START/PAUSE to begin cooking. 6. When cooking is complete, gently flip prawns and cook for an additional 4 minutes. 7. Transfer cooked prawns to a large plate and serve with cocktail sauce.
Per Serving: Calories 411; Fat 5.12g; Sodium 2140mg; Carbs 70.92g; Fibre 2.4g; Sugar 32.21g; Protein 22.35g

Lemony Sea bass

Prep Time: 10 minutes | Cook Time: 15 minutes | Serves: 3

200 g sea bass, trimmed
4 lemon slices
1 tablespoon thyme
2 teaspoons sesame oil
1 teaspoon salt

1. Fill the sea bass with lemon slices and rub with salt, thyme, and sesame oil. 2. Install a crisper plate in both baskets, place the fish in the baskets, and insert the baskets into the unit. Select Zone 1, select AIR FRY, set temperature to 195°C, and set time to 12 minutes. Select MATCH COOK to match Zone 2 settings to Zone 1. Press the START/PAUSE button to begin cooking. 3. Press the START/PAUSE button to flip the fish on another side and cook it for 3 minutes more. 4. When the cooking is complete, remove and serve.
Per Serving: Calories 145; Fat 6.95g; Sodium 842mg; Carbs 4.61g; Fibre 0.3g; Sugar 1.61g; Protein 17.58g

Garlic Prawns with Alfredo Pasta

Prep Time: 10 minutes | Cook Time: 40 minutes | Serves: 4

For the Garlic Prawns:
455 g peeled small prawns, thawed if frozen
1 tablespoon olive oil
1 tablespoon minced garlic
¼ teaspoon sea salt
10 g chopped fresh parsley
For the Pasta Alfredo:
200 g no-boil lasagna noodles
480 ml whole milk
60 g heavy (whipping) cream
2 tablespoons unsalted butter, cut into small pieces
1 tablespoon minced garlic
½ teaspoon salt
¼ teaspoon freshly ground black pepper
50 g grated Parmesan cheese

1. Combine the prawns, garlic, oil, and salt in a large bowl. 2. Break the lasagna noodles into 5 cm pieces and place in a bowl, toss with the cream, garlic, butter, salt, and black pepper. Stir well and ensure the pasta is fully submerged in the liquid. Then transfer to the Zone 2 basket. 3. Install a crisper plate in the Zone 1 basket. Place the prawns in the basket and insert the basket in the unit. Insert the Zone 2 basket in the unit. 4. Select Zone 1, select AIR FRY, set the temperature to 200°C, and set the time for 13 minutes. 5. Select Zone 2, select BAKE, set the temperature to 180°C, and set the time for 40 minutes. Select SMART FINISH. Press START/PAUSE to begin cooking. 6. When the Zone 2 timer reads 20 minutes, press START/PAUSE. Remove the basket and stir the pasta. Reinsert the basket and press START/PAUSE to continue cooking. 7. When cooking is complete, transfer the pasta to a serving dish and stir in the Parmesan. Top with the prawns and parsley.
Per Serving: Calories 416; Fat 18.54g; Sodium 1457mg; Carbs 36.08g; Fibre 0.3g; Sugar 15.96g; Protein 25.66g

Crunchy Haddock Sticks

Prep Time: 15 minutes | Cook Time: 11 minutes | Serves: 4

Salt and pepper
680 g skinless haddock fillets, 2 cm thick, sliced into 10 cm strips
210 g panko bread crumbs
1 tablespoon vegetable oil
30 g plain flour
60 g mayonnaise
2 large eggs
2 tablespoons Dijon mustard
1 tablespoon Old Bay seasoning

1. In a large container, add 70 g salt and 1.8 L of cold water and stir until the salt dissolves. Add haddock, cover, and let sit for 15 minutes. 2. In a bowl, mix up the panko and oil and microwave, stirring often, until light golden brown, 2 to 4 minutes; transfer to shallow dish. In a separate bowl, whisk together the flour, eggs, mayonnaise, Old Bay, mustard, ⅛ teaspoon salt, and ⅛ teaspoon pepper. 3. Set a wire rack in rimmed baking sheet and spray with vegetable oil spray. Remove the haddock from brine and pat dry with paper towels. One piece at a time, dredge the haddock in egg mixture first and drip off any excess, then coat with the panko mixture, pressing gently to adhere. Transfer fish sticks to the prepared rack and freeze until firm, about 1 hour. 4. Install a crisper plate in the Zone 1 basket and lightly spray with vegetable oil spray. Place the fish sticks in the basket, spaced evenly apart and insert the basket in the unit. Lightly spray base of air-fryer basket with vegetable oil spray. Arrange up to 5 fish sticks in prepared basket, spaced evenly apart. (If one basket can't fit so much food, you can choose to cook with the Zone 2 basket and use the MATCH COOK mode) 5. Select Zone 1, select AIR FRY, set the temperature to 205°C, and set time for 11 minutes. Press START/PAUSE to begin cooking. 6. Flip halfway through the cooking time. Serve.

Per Serving: Calories 313; Fat 12.15g; Sodium 829mg; Carbs 16.17g; Fibre 1.3g; Sugar 1.26g; Protein 32.68g

Chapter 6 Snacks and Starters

Easy Beef Meatballs ………………………………………… 51

Flavourful Sweet Potato Fries…………………………………… 51

Buffalo Cauliflower…………………………………………… 51

Savoury Spiced Pork Ribs ………………………………………… 52

Homemade Peanut Butter Oats Poppers ……………………………… 52

Easy Parmesan Chips ……………………………………………… 52

Spiced Cashew Nuts ……………………………………………… 53

Crunchy Onion Rings ……………………………………………… 53

Crisp Kale Chips…………………………………………………… 53

Savoury Meatballs in Tomato Sauce ……………………………… 54

Spicy Breaded Cheese Sticks ……………………………………… 54

Parmesan Cauliflower Dip ………………………………………… 55

Homemade Crab Croquettes ……………………………………… 55

Easy Beef Meatballs

Prep time: 15 minutes | Cook time: 20 minutes | Serves: 6

280g beef mince
1 tablespoon dried coriander
1 egg, beaten
1 teaspoon ground black pepper

1. Mix all remaining ingredients and make the meatballs from them. 2. Insert the crisper plates in the baskets. 3. Divide the meatballs between the baskets in zone 1 and zone 2. 4. Select ROAST mode, adjust the cooking temperature to 185°C and set the cooking time to 20 minutes. 5. Press the MATCH COOK button and copy the zone 1 settings to zone 2. 6. Press the START/PAUSE button to begin cooking. 7. Serve hot.
Per Serving: Calories 185; Fat 10.01g; Sodium 63mg; Carbs 0.48g; Fibre 0.1g; Sugar 0.11g; Protein 21.67g

Flavourful Sweet Potato Fries

Prep Time: 5 minutes | Cook Time: 15 minutes | Serves: 3

2 large-sized sweet potatoes, peeled and cut into 1-cm thick sticks
2 teaspoons olive oil
1 teaspoon garlic powder
1 tablespoon Mediterranean herb mix
Salt and freshly ground black pepper, to taste

1. Toss the sweet potato with the remaining ingredients. Install a crisper plate in both baskets, place the sweet potatoes in the baskets, and insert the baskets into the unit. 2. Select Zone 1, select AIR FRY, set temperature to 180°C, and set time to 15 minutes. Select MATCH COOK to match Zone 2 settings to Zone 1. Press the START/PAUSE button to begin cooking. 3. Press the START/PAUSE button to toss halfway through the cooking time. 4. When the cooking is complete, remove and serve. Enjoy!
Per Serving: Calories 141; Fat 3.21g; Sodium 433mg; Carbs 26.48g; Fibre 4.2g; Sugar 7.91g; Protein 2.66g

Buffalo Cauliflower

Prep Time: 15 minutes. | Cook Time: 14 minutes. | Servings: 4

1 cauliflower head, cut into florets
1 tablespoon butter, melted
120ml buffalo sauce
Black pepper
Salt

1. In a suitable bowl, mix together buffalo sauce, butter, black pepper, and salt. 2. Install a crisper plate in the Zone 1 basket and grease it with cooking spray. Place the cauliflower florets inside. Then, insert the basket in the unit. Select Zone 1, select AIR FRY, set the temperature to 200°C, and set the time for 7 minutes. Press START/PAUSE to begin cooking. 3. Transfer cauliflower florets into the buffalo sauce mixture and toss well. Again, add cauliflower florets into the air fryer basket and cook for 7 minutes more at 200°C. 4. Serve with your favourite dipping sauce.

Chapter 6 Snacks and Starters

Savoury Spiced Pork Ribs

Prep Time: 5 minutes | Cook Time: 35 minutes | Serves: 4

900 g pork ribs
2 tablespoons honey
2 tablespoons butter
1 teaspoon sweet paprika
1 teaspoon hot paprika
1 teaspoon granulated garlic
Sea salt and ground black pepper, to taste
1 teaspoon brown mustard
1 teaspoon ground cumin

1. Install a crisper plate in both baskets. Toss all ingredients in the lightly greased baskets. 2. Insert the baskets into the unit. Select Zone 1, select AIR FRY, set temperature to 175°C, and set time to 35 minutes. Select MATCH COOK to match Zone 2 settings to Zone 1. Press the START/PAUSE button to begin cooking. 3. Press the START/PAUSE button to turn them over halfway through the cooking time. 4. When the cooking is complete, remove and serve. Bon appétit!
Per Serving: Calories 412; Fat 18.88g; Sodium 214mg; Carbs 10.88g; Fibre 0.7g; Sugar 9.35g; Protein 47.75g

Homemade Peanut Butter Oats Poppers

Prep Time: 10 minutes | Cook Time: 8 minutes | Serves: 10

120 g unsweetened applesauce
260 g peanut butter
180 g oats
120 g flour
1 tsp. baking powder

1. In a bowl, combine the applesauce and peanut butter and mix until smooth. 2. Pour in the flour, oats, and baking powder. Continue mixing to form a soft dough. 3. Shape a half-teaspoon of dough into a ball and repeat with the remaining dough. 4. Install a crisper plate in both baskets and grease them with oil. 5. Place the poppers evenly in the baskets and insert the baskets in the unit. Select Zone 1, select AIR FRY, set the temperature to 200°C, and set the time to 8 minutes. Select MATCH COOK to match Zone 2 settings to Zone 1. Press the START/PAUSE button to begin cooking. Flip the balls halfway through the cooking time. 6. Let the poppers cool and serve immediately or keep in an airtight container for up to 2 weeks.
Per Serving: Calories 171; Fat 6.07g; Sodium 387mg; Carbs 29.94g; Fibre 3.9g; Sugar 6.37g; Protein 6.38g

Easy Parmesan Chips

Prep time: 5 minutes | Cook time: 5 minutes | Serves: 4

150g Parmesan, grated

1. Make the small circles from the grated cheese. 2. Insert the crisper plate in the basket in zone 1, and transfer the food to it. 3. Select AIR FRY mode, adjust the cooking temperature to 205°C and set the cooking time to 5 minutes. 4. Press the START/PAUSE button to begin cooking. 5. Cool the Parmesan chips before serving.
Per Serving: Calories 139; Fat 1.88g; Sodium 431mg; Carbs 15g; Fiber 0g; Sugar 0.56g; Protein 15g

Chapter 6 Snacks and Starters

Spiced Cashew Nuts

Prep Time: 15 minutes | Cook Time: 15 minutes | Serves: 3

275 g cashew nuts
½ tsp. garam masala powder
1 tsp. coriander powder
1 tsp. ghee
1 tsp. red chili powder
½ tsp. black pepper
2 tsp. dry mango powder
1 tsp. sea salt

1. Combine all the ingredients in a bowl and toss well. 2. Install a crisper plate in the Zone 1 basket. Place the seasoned cashew nuts in the basket and insert the basket in the unit. 3. Select Zone 1, select AIR FRY, set the temperature to 120°C, and set time for 15 minutes. Press START/PAUSE to begin cooking. Cook until the nuts are brown and crispy. 4. Let the nuts cool before serving or transfer to an airtight container to be stored for up to 2 weeks.
Per Serving: Calories 436; Fat 34.72g; Sodium 811mg; Carbs 24.3g; Fibre 3.3g; Sugar 4.56g; Protein 14.18g

Crunchy Onion Rings

Prep Time: 10 minutes | Cook Time: 10 minutes | Serves: 2

1 large onion, cut into slices
1 egg, beaten
75 g bread crumbs
240 ml milk
1 tsp. baking powder
155 g flour
1 tsp. salt

1. In a small bowl, mix together the flour, baking powder, and salt. 2. In another bowl, whisk the egg and milk. 3. Place the bread crumbs in a shallow dish. 4. Dip each slice of onion with the flour, then dredge it in the egg mixture. Finally, press it into the breadcrumbs. 5. Install a crisper plate in the Zone 1 basket. Place the coated onion rings in the basket and insert the basket in the unit. 6. Select Zone 1, select AIR FRY, set the temperature to 175°C, and set the time for 10 minutes. Press START/PAUSE to begin cooking. 7. When cooking is complete, serve immediately.
Per Serving: Calories 491; Fat 10.1g; Sodium 1338mg; Carbs 80.65g; Fibre 3.8g; Sugar 10.62g; Protein 18.39g

Crisp Kale Chips

Prep Time: 15 minutes | Cook Time: 5 minutes | Servings: 4

85g kale, stemmed
1 tablespoon nutritional yeast flakes
2 teaspoon ranch seasoning
2 tablespoons olive oil
¼ teaspoon salt

1. Add all the recipe ingredients into the suitable mixing bowl and toss well. 2. Install a crisper plate in the Zone 1 basket and grease it with cooking spray. Place the kale inside. Then, insert the basket in the unit. Select Zone 1, select AIR FRY, set the temperature to 185°C, and set the time for 5 minutes. Press START/PAUSE to begin cooking. 3. Serve and enjoy.

Savoury Meatballs in Tomato Sauce

Prep Time: 15 minutes | Cook Time: 23 minutes | Serves: 4

1 small onion, finely chopped
300 g beef mince
1 tbsp. chopped fresh parsley
½ tbsp. chopped fresh thyme leaves
1 egg
3 tbsp. friendly bread crumbs
Pepper and salt to taste
250 g your favorite tomato sauce if desired

1. Add all the ingredients in a bowl except the tomato sauce and mix well. Shape the mixture into 10 - 12 balls with your hands. 2. Install a crisper plate in both baskets. Place the meatballs evenly in the baskets and insert the baskets in the unit. 3. Select Zone 1, select AIR FRY, set the temperature to 200°C, and set the time to 18 minutes. Select MATCH COOK to match Zone 2 settings to Zone 1. Press the START/PAUSE button to begin cooking. 4. When cooking time is up, remove the baskets and transfer the meatballs to a baking dish that fits the air fryer basket, pour in the tomato sauce and set the dish in the zone 1 basket of the Air Fryer. 5. Lower the temperature to 165°C and warm the meatballs for 5 minutes.

Per Serving: Calories 169; Fat 5.4g; Sodium 204mg; Carbs 23.53g; Fibre 2.5g; Sugar 5.92g; Protein 7.31g

Spicy Breaded Cheese Sticks

Prep Time: 15 minutes | Cook Time: 5 minutes | Serves: 4

455 g mozzarella cheese
2 eggs, beaten
1 tsp. cayenne pepper
100 g bread crumbs
1 tsp. onion powder
1 tsp. garlic powder
125 g flour
½ tsp. salt

1. Slice the mozzarella cheese into 3- x 1 cm sticks. 2. Whisk the eggs in a bowl. Place the flour into a shallow dish. 3. In another bowl, mix together the bread crumbs, onion powder, garlic powder, cayenne pepper, and salt. 4. Dredge the mozzarella strips in the egg, then dredge it in the flour. Dip it in the egg again. Finally, press it into the bread crumbs. Refrigerate for 20 minutes. 5. Install a crisper plate in the Zone 1 basket and spray with cooking spray. Place the coated cheese sticks in the basket and insert it in the unit. 6. Select Zone 1, select AIR FRY, set the temperature to 205°C, and set the time for 5 minutes. Press START/PAUSE to begin cooking. 7. Serve immediately.

Per Serving: Calories 368; Fat 5.51g; Sodium 1229mg; Carbs 33.94g; Fibre 3.4g; Sugar 2.69g; Protein 44.68g

Parmesan Cauliflower Dip

Prep Time: 15 minutes. | Cook Time: 32 minutes. | Servings: 10

1 cauliflower head, cut into florets
150g parmesan cheese, shredded
2 tablespoons green onions, chopped
2 garlic clove
1 teaspoon Worcestershire sauce
115g sour cream
190g mayonnaise
225g cream cheese, softened
2 tablespoons olive oil

1. Toss cauliflower florets with olive oil. 2. Install a crisper plate in the Zone 1 basket and place the cauliflower florets inside. Then, insert the basket in the unit. Select Zone 1, select AIR FRY, set the temperature to 200°C, and set the time for 20 minutes. Press START/PAUSE to begin cooking. 3. Add cooked cauliflower, 100g of parmesan cheese, green onion, garlic, Worcestershire sauce, sour cream, mayonnaise, and cream cheese into the food processor and process until smooth. 4. Transfer the cauliflower mixture to a round baking dish and top with the remaining parmesan cheese. 5. Place the dish in Zone 1 basket and Cook at 180°C for 12 minutes. 6. Serve and enjoy.

Homemade Crab Croquettes

Prep Time: 15 minutes | Cook Time: 14 minutes | Serves: 6

For the Filling:
455 g lump crab meat
2 egg whites, beaten
1 tbsp. olive oil
30 g red onion, finely chopped
¼ red pepper, finely chopped
2 tbsp. celery, finely chopped
¼ tsp. tarragon, finely chopped
¼ tsp. chives, finely chopped
½ tsp. parsley, finely chopped
½ tsp. cayenne pepper
60 g mayonnaise
60 g sour cream
For the Breading:
3 eggs, beaten
120 g flour
100 g
100 g friendly bread crumbs
1 tsp. olive oil
½ tsp. salt

1. In a pan over medium heat, sauté the olive oil, peppers, onions, and celery. Cook until the vegetables turn translucent, about 4 - 5 minutes. 2. Remove from the heat and set aside to cool. 3. Pulse the bread crumbs, olive oil and salt in a food processor to form a fine crumb. 4. Whisk the eggs in a bowl; place the panko mixture in a second bowl; place the flour in a third bowl. 5. In a large bowl, mix together the crabmeat, egg whites, sour cream, mayonnaise, spices and vegetables. 6. Shape the crab mixture into several golf- sized balls. Coat the balls in the flour, then dip them in the eggs and finally in the panko. 7. Install a crisper plate in both baskets. Put croquettes evenly in both baskets in a single layer and well-spaced. Then insert the basket in the unit. 8. Select Zone 1, select AIR FRY, set the temperature to 200°C, and set the time to 9 minutes. Select MATCH COOK to match Zone 2 settings to Zone 1. Press the START/PAUSE button to begin cooking. Cook until a golden brown colour is achieved.
Per Serving: Calories 474; Fat 14.72g; Sodium 388mg; Carbs 50.26g; Fibre 14.3g; Sugar 1.3g; Protein 38.24g

Chapter 7 Desserts

Homemade Chocolate Cake 57

Cinnamon Hazelnut Cookies 57

Air Fryer Chocolate Chip Cookies 58

Cinnamon Walnuts & Raisins Stuffed Apples 58

Mini Apple Pies 59

Easy Blueberry Pie 59

Delicious Cherry Cobbler 60

Coconut Chocolate Fudgy Brownies 60

Peanut Butter Chocolate Fudge Cake 61

Pecan Chocolate Cake... 61

Cinnamon Pineapple Slices 62

Coconut Cookies... 62

Ricotta Cheese Cake 63

Ice Cream Profiteroles with Chocolate Sauce.......................... 63

Lemony Doughnuts... 64

Homemade Chocolate Cake

Prep Time: 15 minutes | Cook Time: 15 minutes | Serves: 6

55 g butter, at room temperature
100 g chocolate, unsweetened and chopped
1 tablespoon liquid stevia
160 g coconut flour
A pinch of fine sea salt
2 eggs, whisked
½ teaspoon vanilla extract

1. Microwave the butter, chocolate, and stevia in a microwave-safe bowl until melted. 2. Let it cool for a few minutes and add the remaining ingredients; stir to combine well. Scrape the batter into a lightly greased baking pan that fits the air fryer basket. Place the pan in the Zone 1 basket and insert the basket in the unit. 3. Select Zone 1, select AIR FRY, set the temperature to 165°C, and set time for 15 minutes. Press START/PAUSE to begin cooking. 4. Bake until the centre is springy and a toothpick comes out dry. Enjoy!
Per Serving: Calories 194; Fat 11.33g; Sodium 310mg; Carbs 18.96g; Fibre 1.3g; Sugar 14.25g; Protein 4.07g

Cinnamon Hazelnut Cookies

Prep time: 60 minutes | Cook time: 15 minutes | Serves: 10

4 tablespoons liquid monk fruit
60g hazelnuts, ground
115g butter, room temperature
200g almond flour
120g coconut flour
50g granulated sweetener
2 teaspoons ground cinnamon

1. Cream liquid monk fruit with butter until the mixture becomes fluffy. Sift in both types of flour. 2. Stir in the hazelnuts. Knead the mixture to form dough; place in the refrigerator to chill it for about 35 minutes. 3. Shape the prepared dough into the bite-sized balls; arrange them on a baking dish; flatten the balls using the back of a spoon. 4. Mix granulated sweetener with ground cinnamon. Press the cookies in the cinnamon mixture until they are completely covered. 5. Insert the crisper plates in the baskets and line them with parchment paper. 6. Divide the cookies between the baskets in zone 1 and zone 2. 7. Select BAKE mode, adjust the cooking temperature to 155°C and set the cooking time to 20 minutes. 8. Press the MATCH COOK button and copy the zone 1 settings to zone 2. 9. Press the START/PAUSE button to begin cooking. 10. Leave them to cool for about 10 minutes before serving.
Per Serving: Calories 157; Fat 13.44g; Sodium 98mg; Carbs 9.34g; Fibre 1.3g; Sugar 7.72g; Protein 1.37g

Air Fryer Chocolate Chip Cookies

Prep Time: 10 minutes | Cook Time: 5 minutes | Serves: 5

220 g unsalted butter, at room temperature
200 g granulated sugar
210 g brown sugar
2 large eggs
½ teaspoon vanilla extract
1 teaspoon baking soda
½ teaspoon salt
375 g plain flour
200 g chocolate chips

1. Cream the butter and both sugars in a large bowl. 2. Whisk in the eggs, vanilla, salt, flour and baking soda until well combined. Fold in the chocolate chips. 3. Knead the mixture into dough with your hands. 4. Install a crisper plate in both baskets and spray with cooking spray. Drop heaping spoonfuls of dough onto the baskets bout 2.5 cm apart with a cookie scoop. Then insert the baskets in the unit. 5. Select Zone 1, select AIR FRY, set the temperature to 170°C, and set time to 5 minutes. Select MATCH COOK to match Zone 2 settings to Zone 1. Press the START/PAUSE button to begin cooking. 6. When the cookies are golden brown and cooked through, use silicone oven mitts to remove the baking sheet from the air fryer and serve.

Per Serving: Calories 1014; Fat 54.84g; Sodium 519mg; Carbs 112.44g; Fibre 10.8g; Sugar 39.9g; Protein 17.87g

Cinnamon Walnuts & Raisins Stuffed Apples

Prep Time: 5 minutes | Cook Time: 20 minutes | Serves: 4

4 to 6 tablespoons chopped walnuts
4 to 6 tablespoons raisins
4 tablespoons unsalted butter, melted
1 teaspoon ground cinnamon
½ teaspoon ground nutmeg
4 apples, cored but with the bottoms left intact
Vanilla ice cream, for topping
Maple syrup, for topping

1. In a small mixing bowl, mix together the walnuts, raisins, cinnamon, melted butter, and nutmeg. 2. Scoop a quarter of the filling into each apple. 3. Place the apples in a baking pan that fits the basket and set the pan in the zone 1 basket. 4. Select Zone 1, select BAKE, set the temperature to 175°C, and set the time for 20 minutes. Press START/PAUSE to begin cooking. 5. Serve with vanilla ice cream and a drizzle of maple syrup.

Per Serving: Calories 364; Fat 14.79g; Sodium 110mg; Carbs 56.45g; Fibre 4.9g; Sugar 33.78g; Protein 5.83g

Mini Apple Pies

Prep Time: 10 minutes | Cook Time: 4 minutes | Serves: 8

1 package prepared pie dough
90 g apple pie filling
1 large egg white
1 tablespoon Sugar
Caramel sauce, for drizzling

1. Lay out the dough on a floured work surface. 2. Cut out 8 circles from the dough with a 5 cm biscuit cutter. 3. Gather up the dough pieces and knead form them into a ball, and reroll them up again. Use a cookie knife to cut out the remaining dough. 4. Add about 1 tablespoon of apple pie filling to the centre of each circle. 5. Fold over the dough and use a fork to seal the edges. 6. Brush the egg white over the top and sprinkle with sparkling sugar. 7. Install a crisper plate in both baskets and spray with olive oil. Place the hand pies evenly in both baskets. They should be spaced so that they do not touch one another. Then insert the baskets in the unit. 8. Select Zone 1, select BAKE, set the temperature to 175°C, and set time to 2 minutes. Select MATCH COOK to match Zone 2 settings to Zone 1. Press the START/PAUSE button to begin cooking. 9. When cooking is complete, the crust should be golden brown. If not, bake for another 2 minutes. Drizzle with caramel sauce, if desired.
Per Serving: Calories 230; Fat 11.19g; Sodium 307mg; Carbs 29.91g; Fibre 0.4g; Sugar 6.79g; Protein 2.97g

Easy Blueberry Pie

Prep Time: 15 minutes | Cook Time: 15 minutes | Serves: 6

2 frozen pie crusts
2 jars blueberry pie filling
1 teaspoon milk
1 teaspoon sugar

1. Remove the pie crusts from the freezer and let them sit on the countertop for 30 minutes. 2. Place one crust into the bottom of a pie pan. Spread the filling on the bottom crust and cover it with another crust, taking care to press the edges of the bottom and upper crust together to form a seal. 3. Trim off excess pie dough. 4. Cut out the venting holes in the top crust with a knife. 5. Brush the top crust with milk, then sprinkle the sugar. 6. Install a crisper plate in the Zone 1 basket. Place the pie in the basket and insert in the unit. 7. Select Zone 1, select BAKE, set the temperature to 155°C, and set the time for 15 minutes. Press START/PAUSE to begin cooking. 8. Check the pie after 15 minutes. If it needs additional time, reset the timer and bake for 3 minutes more. 9. Remove the pie from the air fryer with a silicone oven mitt. Let cool for 15 minutes before serving.
Per Serving: Calories 633; Fat 14.31g; Sodium 301mg; Carbs 123.07g; Fibre 6.4g; Sugar 86.99g; Protein 2.81g

Delicious Cherry Cobbler

Prep Time: 10 minutes | Cook Time: 25 minutes | Serves: 4

125 g plain flour
200 g sugar
2 tablespoons baking powder
180 ml milk
8 tablespoons unsalted butter
1 can cherry pie filling

1. Mix together the flour, sugar, and baking powder in a small mixing bowl. Stir in the milk and mix until well blended. 2. Add butter to a microwave-safe bowl. Microwave for about 45 seconds. 3. Pour the butter into the bottom of a pan that fits the air fryer basket. Pour in the batter and spread it in an even layer. Pour the pie filing over the batter. Do not mix; the batter will bubble up through the filling during cooking. 4. Install a crisper plate in the Zone 1 basket. Place the pan in the basket and insert it in the unit. 5. Select Zone 1, select BAKE, set the temperature to 160°C, and set the time for 25 minutes. Press START/PAUSE to begin cooking. 6. Check the cobbler. When the cobbler is done the batter will be golden brown and cooked through. 7. Remove from the air fryer and let cool slightly before serving.

Per Serving: Calories 557; Fat 17.36g; Sodium 64mg; Carbs 96.17g; Fibre 1.9g; Sugar 26.85g; Protein 6.15g

Coconut Chocolate Fudgy Brownies

Prep Time: 15 minutes | Cook Time: 20 minutes | Serves: 8

110 g butter, melted
75 g sweetener
2 eggs
1 teaspoon vanilla essence
2 tablespoons flaxseed meal
100 g coconut flour
1 teaspoon baking powder
40 g cocoa powder, unsweetened
A pinch of salt
A pinch of ground cardamom

1. Spritz the sides and bottom of a baking pan that fits the air fryer basket with cooking spray. 2. Combine the melted butter with sweetener in a bowl and beat until fluffy. Whisk in the eggs and beat again. 3. Then, add the flour, baking powder, vanilla, cocoa, salt, and ground cardamom. Stir until well combined. 4. Pour this mixture into the prepared pan and place the pan in the Zone 1 basket. Then insert the basket in the unit. 5. Select Zone 1, select BAKE, set the temperature to 180°C, and set time for 20 minutes. Press START/PAUSE to begin cooking. Enjoy!

Per Serving: Calories 216; Fat 15.74g; Sodium 296mg; Carbs 18.25g; Fibre 2.7g; Sugar 13.38g; Protein 4.05g

Peanut Butter Chocolate Fudge Cake

Prep time: 30 minutes | Cook time: 22 minutes | Serves: 10

250g peanut butter
225g monk fruit
3 eggs
100g almond flour
1 teaspoon baking powder
¼ teaspoon salt
140g cooking chocolate, broken into chunks

1. Spritz the sides and bottom of a suitable baking pan with cooking spray. 2. Thoroughly combine the peanut butter with the monk fruit in the pan until creamy. Fold in the egg and beat until fluffy. 3. Stir in the almond flour, baking powder, salt, and bakers' chocolate. Mix them until everything is well combined. 4. Transfer the pan to the basket in zone 1. 5. Select BAKE mode, adjust the cooking temperature to 175°C and set the cooking time to 22 minutes. 6. Press the START/PAUSE button to begin cooking. 7. Transfer the pan to a wire rack to cool the dish before slicing and serving.
Per Serving: Calories 279; Fat 18.84g; Sodium 90mg; Carbs 21.17g; Fiber 4g; Sugar 12.69g; Protein 10.24g

Pecan Chocolate Cake

Prep time: 30 minutes | Cook time: 22 minutes | Serves: 6

115g butter, melted
15g sweetener
1 teaspoon vanilla essence
1 egg
50g almond flour
½ teaspoon baking powder
25g cocoa powder
½ teaspoon ground cinnamon
¼ teaspoon fine sea salt
25g cooking chocolate, unsweetened
30g pecans, finely chopped

1. Lightly grease six silicone molds. 2. In a mixing dish, beat the melted butter with the sweetener until fluffy. Stir in the vanilla and egg and beat again. 3. Add the almond flour, baking powder, cocoa powder, cinnamon, and salt. Mix them until everything is well combined. 4. Fold in the chocolate and pecans; mix to combine. 5. Divide them among the molds. 6. Insert the crisper plates in the baskets. Divide the molds between the baskets in zone 1 and zone 2. 7. Select BAKE mode, adjust the cooking temperature to 175°C and set the cooking time to 22 minutes. 8. Press the MATCH COOK button and copy the zone 1 settings to zone 2. 9. Press the START/PAUSE button to begin cooking. 10. Serve warm.
Per Serving: Calories 210; Fat 20.5g; Sodium 240mg; Carbs 6.4g; Fibre 1.7g; Sugar 2.79g; Protein 2.81g

Cinnamon Pineapple Slices

Prep Time: 15 minutes. | Cook Time: 20 minutes. | Servings: 4

4 pineapple slices
1 teaspoon cinnamon
2 tablespoon erythritol

1. Add pineapple slices, sweetener, and cinnamon into the zip-lock bag. 2. Shake well and keep in the refrigerator for 30 minutes. 3. Install a crisper plate in the Zone 1 basket and place the pineapple slices inside. Then, insert the basket in the unit. Select Zone 1, select AIR FRY, set the temperature to 175°C, and set the time for 20 minutes. Press START/PAUSE to begin cooking. Turn halfway through. 4. Serve and enjoy.

Coconut Cookies

Prep time: 20 minutes | Cook time: 10 minutes | Serves: 12

230g butter, melted
50g granulated sweetener
3 eggs
2 tablespoons coconut milk
1 teaspoon coconut extract
1 teaspoon vanilla extract
120g coconut flour
125g almond flour
½ teaspoon baking powder
½ teaspoon baking soda
½ teaspoon fine table salt
50g coconut chips, unsweetened

1. In the bowl of an electric mixer, beat the butter and sweetener until well combined. Now, add the eggs one at a time, and mix well; add the coconut milk, coconut extract, and vanilla; beat until creamy and uniform. 2. Mix the flour with baking powder, baking soda, and salt. Then, stir the flour mixture into the butter mixture and stir until everything is well incorporated. 3. Fold in the coconut chips and mix again. Scoop out 1 tablespoon size balls of the batter on a cookie pan, leaving 5 cm between each cookie. 4. BAKE the food in both zones at 175°C for 10 minutes, flipping them once or twice during cooking. 5. Let the cookies cool on wire racks.
Per Serving: Calories 232; Fat 21.92g; Sodium 305mg; Carbs 6.32g; Fiber 1.5g; Sugar 3.89g; Protein 3.94g

Chapter 7 Desserts

Ricotta Cheese Cake

Prep Time: 15 minutes. | Cook Time: 30 minutes. | Servings: 8

3 eggs, beaten
1 teaspoon baking powder
100g ghee, melted
110g almond flour
65g erythritol
245g ricotta cheese, soft

1. Add all the recipe ingredients into the bowl and mix until well combined. 2. Pour batter into a greased, round baking pan. 3. Place the pan in the Zone 1 basket, then insert the basket in the unit. Select Zone 1, select BAKE, set the temperature to 175°C, and set the time for 30 minutes. Press START/PAUSE to begin cooking. 4. Slice and serve with your favourite fruits.

Ice Cream Profiteroles with Chocolate Sauce

Prep Time: 10 minutes | Cook Time: 17 minutes | Serves: 4-5

Choux Puffs:
3 tablespoons unsalted butter
1 tablespoon granulated sugar
235 ml water
125 g plain flour
2 eggs
Vegetable oil for brushing

Chocolate Sauce:
115 g semisweet chocolate, finely chopped
30 g unsalted butter at room temperature
240 ml heavy cream
85 g corn syrup
285 g vanilla ice cream for serving

1. Add the sugar, butter and water in a medium saucepan and melt the butter at low heat. Add the flour to stir to form a cohesive dough. Cook over medium-low heat for 2 minutes to get rid of the raw flour taste. Remove from the heat and let cool to room temperature. Beat the eggs in one at a time, ensuring the first egg is fully incorporated before the adding the second. The dough will look curdled at first, but keep beating vigorously until the dough becomes smooth. Once the eggs are fully mixed, let the dough rest for 30 minutes. 2. While the dough is resting, make the chocolate sauce. Place the chopped chocolate and butter in a heat-proof bowl. Heat the corn syrup and cream in a saucepan at medium heat until the cream is simmering. Remove from the heat and pour the cream mixture over the chocolate in the bowl. Stir until the mixture is melted and the sauce is smooth. Set aside. 3. Once the dough has rested, place it in a piping bag outfitted with a large, round tip. Install a crisper plate in both baskets. Lightly oil the baskets. Working in 2 batches, pipe round puffs of dough approximately 5 cm wide and 2.5 cm tall directly onto the baskets. Use a knife or scissors to cut the dough when achieved the desired size. With a damp finger, press down on the swirl at the top of each puff to round it. 4. Insert the baskets into the unit. Select Zone 1, select AIR FRY, set temperature to 180°C, and set time to 20 minutes. Select MATCH COOK to match Zone 2 settings to Zone 1, and press the START/PAUSE button to begin cooking until the outside of the puffs is golden brown and crisp and the inside is fully cooked and airy. 5. When the cooking is complete, halve the choux puffs crosswise and place a scoop of ice cream inside each one. Replace the top of the puff and spoon chocolate sauce over the top. Serve immediately.

Per Serving: Calories 567; Fat 29.46g; Sodium 163mg; Carbs 66.82g; Fibre 1.6g; Sugar 37.77g; Protein 10.41g

Chapter 7 Desserts | 63

Lemony Doughnuts

Prep Time: 15 minutes | Cook Time: 6 minutes | Serves: 6-8

120 ml milk, warmed to between 38°C to 43°C
1 teaspoon yeast
50 g granulated sugar, divided
250 g plain flour
½ teaspoon salt
Zest and juice of 1 lemon
4 tablespoons (55 g) unsalted butter, melted
1 egg
Vegetable oil for spraying
150 g icing sugar, sifted
Dried lavender for culinary use (optional)

1. Combine the yeast, warm milk, and a pinch of the sugar in a small bowl and whisk to mix. Allow to sit until the yeast blooms and looks bubbly, about 5 to 10 minutes. Meanwhile, whisk together the flour, remaining sugar, and salt. Add the zest of the lemon to the dry ingredients. 2. When the yeast has bloomed, add the milk mixture to the dry ingredients to stir to combine well. Add the egg and melted butter to stir to form a thick dough. Place the dough onto a well-floured board and knead until smooth, 1 to 2 minutes. Place the dough in an oiled bowl, then cover, and allow to rise in the refrigerator overnight. 3. The next day, remove the dough from the refrigerator and allow it to come to room temperature. Turn the risen dough out onto a well-floured board. Roll the dough out until it is approximately 6 mm thick. Using a 7.5 or 10 cm circular cookie cutter, cut out as many doughnuts as possible. Use a 2.5 cm round cookie cutter to cut out holes from the centre of each doughnut. With the dough scraps, you can either cut out additional doughnut holes using the 2.5 cm cutter or, if desired, gather the scraps and roll them out again to cut out more doughnuts. 4. Transfer the doughnuts and doughnut holes to a lined baking sheet. Cover with a clean kitchen towel and let proof in a warm place until puffy and, when pressed with a finger, the dough slowly springs back, 30 minutes to 1 hour. 5. While the dough is proofing, make the glaze. Whisk together the sifted powdered sugar and the juice from the lemon in a bowl. Set aside. 6. Install a crisper plate in both baskets. When the doughnuts have proofed, spray the baskets with oil. Transfer no more than 3 or 4 of the doughnuts and 2 or 3 of the holes to the baskets. Spray the doughnuts lightly with oil. Insert place the baskets into the unit. Select Zone 1, select AIR FRY, set temperature to 180°C, and set time to 6 minutes. Select MATCH COOK to match Zone 2 settings to Zone 1. Press the START/PAUSE button to begin cooking. 7. Press the START/PAUSE button to flip once halfway through until browned and cooked through. 8. When the cooking is complete, transfer the cooked doughnuts and holes to a cooling rack. 9. Once the doughnuts are cool enough to handle, dip the tops into the glaze. Return the dipped doughnuts to the rack to allow the excess glaze to drip off. Once the glaze has hardened, dip each doughnut again to create a nice opaque finish. While the second glaze is still wet if desired, sprinkle a few buds of lavender over each doughnut.
Per Serving: Calories 303; Fat 7.16g; Sodium 218mg; Carbs 53.28g; Fibre 1g; Sugar 25.71g; Protein 6.01g

Conclusion

As we near the end of our culinary adventure with the "Ninja Foodi Dual Air Fryer Cookbook," it's evident that this kitchen marvel has the potential to completely revolutionize your cooking experience. The Ninja Foodi Dual Air Fryer is a game changer in modern cooking, from its unique features to the numerous benefits it provides. We've equipped you to master this appliance and raise your cooking talents with our step-by-step guidance, insightful hints, and answers to your queries. So go forth and explore, experiment, and enjoy the world of flavours that this extraordinary technology unlocks. With the Ninja Foodi Dual Air Fryer on your side, your culinary adventures will be nothing short of fantastic. Good luck in the kitchen!

Appendix 1 Measurement Conversion Chart

VOLUME EQUIVALENTS (LIQUID)

US STANDARD	US STANDARD (OUNCES)	METRIC (APPROXIMATE)
2 tablespoons	1 fl.oz	30 mL
¼ cup	2 fl.oz	60 mL
½ cup	4 fl.oz	120 mL
1 cup	8 fl.oz	240 mL
1½ cup	12 fl.oz	355 mL
2 cups or 1 pint	16 fl.oz	475 mL
4 cups or 1 quart	32 fl.oz	1 L
1 gallon	128 fl.oz	4 L

VOLUME EQUIVALENTS (DRY)

US STANDARD	METRIC (APPROXIMATE)
⅛ teaspoon	0.5 mL
¼ teaspoon	1 mL
½ teaspoon	2 mL
¾ teaspoon	4 mL
1 teaspoon	5 mL
1 tablespoon	15 mL
¼ cup	59 mL
½ cup	118 mL
¾ cup	177 mL
1 cup	235 mL
2 cups	475 mL
3 cups	700 mL
4 cups	1 L

TEMPERATURES EQUIVALENTS

FAHRENHEIT(F)	CELSIUS (C) (APPROXIMATE)
225 °F	107 °C
250 °F	120 °C
275 °F	135 °C
300 °F	150 °C
325 °F	160 °C
350 °F	180 °C
375 °F	190 °C
400 °F	205 °C
425 °F	220 °C
450 °F	235 °C
475 °F	245 °C
500 °F	260 °C

WEIGHT EQUIVALENTS

US STANDARD	METRIC (APPROXIMATE)
1 ounce	28 g
2 ounces	57 g
5 ounces	142 g
10 ounces	284 g
15 ounces	425 g
16 ounces (1 pound)	455 g
1.5 pounds	680 g
2 pounds	907 g

Appendix 2 Air Fryer Cooking Char

Frozen Foods	Temp (°F)	Time (min)
Onion Rings (12 oz.)	400	8
Thin French Fries (20 oz.)	400	14
Thick French Fries (17 oz.)	400	18
Pot Sticks (10 oz.)	400	8
Fish Sticks (10 oz.)	400	10
Fish Fillets (½-inch, 10 oz.)	400	14

Vegetables	Temp (°F)	Time (min)
Asparagus (1-inch slices)	400	5
Beets (sliced)	350	25
Beets (whole)	400	40
Bell Peppers (sliced)	350	13
Broccoli	400	6
Brussels Sprouts (halved)	380	15
Carrots (½-inch slices)	380	15
Cauliflower (florets)	400	12
Eggplant (1½-inch cubes)	400	15
Fennel (quartered)	370	15
Mushrooms (¼-inch slices)	400	5
Onion (pearl)	400	10
Parsnips (½-inch chunks)	380	5
Peppers (1-inch chunks)	400	15
Potatoes (baked, whole)	400	40
Squash (½-inch chunks)	400	12
Tomatoes (cherry)	400	4
Zucchni (½-inch sticks)	400	12

Meat	Temp (°F)	Time (min)
Bacon	400	5 to 7
Beef Eye Round Roast (4 lbs.)	390	50 to 60
Burger (4 oz.)	370	16 to 20
Chicken Breasts, bone-in (1.25 lbs.)	370	25
Chicken Breasts, boneless (4 oz.)	380	12
Chicken Drumsticks (2.5 lbs.)	370	20
Chicken Thighs, bone-in (2 lbs.)	380	22
Chicken Thighs, boneless (1.5 lbs.)	380	18 to 20
Chicken Legs, bone-in (1.75 lbs.)	380	30
Chicken Wings (2 lbs.)	400	12
Flank Steak (1.5 lbs.)	400	12
Game Hen (halved, 2 lbs.)	390	20
Loin (2 lbs.)	360	55
London Broil (2 lbs.)	400	20 to 28
Meatballs (3-inch)	380	10
Rack of Lamb (1.5-2 lbs.)	380	22
Sausages	380	15
Whole Chicken (6.5 lbs.)	360	75

Fish and Seafood	Temp (°F)	Time (min)
Calamari (8 oz.)	400	4
Fish Fillet (1-inch, 8 oz.)	400	10
Salmon Fillet (6 oz.)	380	12
Tuna Steak	400	7 to 10
Scallops	400	5 to 7
Shrimp	400	5

Appendix 3 Recipes Index

A

Air Fried Butter Beef Steak 38
Air Fried Pretzels 13
Air Fryer Chocolate Chip Cookies 58
Air Fryer Garlic Aubergine Slices 18

B

Bacon Egg Cups 12
Breaded Crab Croquettes 45
Buffalo Cauliflower 51
Butter Cheese Sandwich 15

C

Cajun Beef Tenderloins 35
Cheese & Pork Rinds-Crusted Chicken Breast 28
Cheese Bacon Muffins 14
Cheese Broccoli Quiche 13
Cheese Mushroom Omelet 21
Cheese Pork Stuffed Peppers 36
Cheese Taquitos with Cilantro 14
Cinnamon Hazelnut Cookies 57
Cinnamon Pineapple Slices 62
Cinnamon Walnuts & Raisins Stuffed Apples 58
Coconut Chocolate Fudgy Brownies 60
Coconut Cookies 62
Corn on the Cob 18
Cornflake-Crusted Chicken Drumsticks 31
Crab Cakes with Capers 42
Crisp Kale Chips 53
Crispy Asparagus with Tarragon 19
Crispy Bacon Slices 39
Crispy Breaded Prawns with Cocktail Sauce 47
Crispy Chicken Cutlets with Lemon-Caper Sauce 30
Crispy Chicken Fillets 23
Crispy Chicken Tenders 24
Crispy Cod Fillets 42
Crispy Corn Croquettes 21
Crispy Fish Fillets 43
Crispy Fish Sticks 44
Crispy Mozzarella Sticks with Salsa 11
Crispy Prawns Scampi 46
Crunchy Breaded Prawn 44
Crunchy Chicken Nuggets 24
Crunchy Haddock Sticks 49
Crunchy Onion Rings 53

D

Delicious Beef Meatloaves 38
Delicious Cherry Cobbler 60
Delicious Hawaiian Butter Beef Rolls 34
Delicious Herb Roasted Whole Chicken 25
Delicious Honey Glazed Halibut Steaks 46
Dill-Turmeric Cauliflower Steaks 19

E

Easy Beef Meatballs 51
Easy Blueberry Pie 59
Easy Parmesan Chips 52
Easy Roasted Broccoli with Spring Onions 17

F

Filet Mignon Steaks with Cream-Garlic Sauce 35
Flank Steak with Potatoes 39
Flavourful Sweet Potato Fries 51

G

Garlic Chicken Sausages 27
Garlic Prawns with Alfredo Pasta 48
Garlicky Courgette Slices 19
Garlicky Mushrooms with Parsley 17
Herbed Garlic Porterhouse Steak 37
Herbed Turkey Breast 26
Homemade Chocolate Cake 57
Homemade Crab Croquettes 55
Homemade Peanut Butter Oats Poppers 52
Homemade Scotch Eggs 12

I

Ice Cream Profiteroles with Chocolate Sauce 63

L

Lemon Rosemary Chicken Wings 26
Lemon Salmon Steaks 43
Lemony Doughnuts 64
Lemony Salmon with Chives 41
Lemony Sea bass 48
Lime Chicken Breast with Parsley 27

M

Meatballs with Tomato Sauce 34
Mini Apple Pies 59
Minty Gruyère Stuffed Mushrooms 11

P

Parmesan Cauliflower Dip 55
Peanut Butter Chocolate Fudge Cake 61
Pecan Chocolate Cake 61
Pecan French Toast with Banana 15
Pickled Chicken Tenders 23

R

Ricotta Cheese Cake 63
Roasted Butternut Squash and Mushrooms with Cranberries 20
Roasted London Broil with Herb Butter 33
Roasted Rosemary Potatoes 17

S

Savoury Beef Hamburgers 37
Savoury Meatballs in Tomato Sauce 54
Savoury Spiced Pork Ribs 52
Savoury Turkey Meatballs with Hoisin Sauce 29
Simple Air Fryer Tilapia 47
Spiced Breaded Potato Wedges 20
Spiced Broccoli in Cheese Sauce 10
Spiced Cashew Nuts 53
Spicy Breaded Cheese Sticks 54
Spicy Coconut Chicken Strips 28
Spicy Garlic Steak 33
Spinach & Tomato Frittata 10
Sweet Potato Fries 18

T

Tasty Air Fryer Sea Bream 45
Tasty Crab & Cauliflower Cakes 41
Tasty Lime Garlic Chicken Wings 25

W

Whisky Sirloin Steak 36

Printed in Great Britain
by Amazon